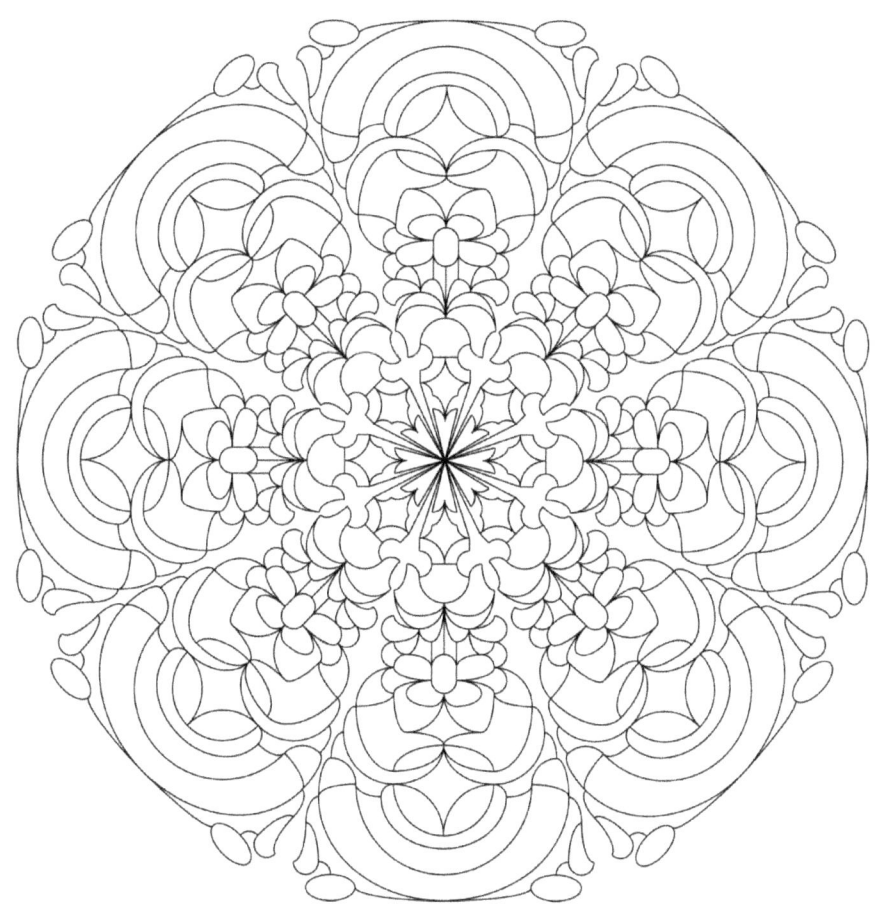

Coloring Designs 3

Kaleidoscopic Mandalas

Colored pencils, markers, and a variety of other media are suitable for use when coloring this book. To help reduce the risk of bleed-through, please place a blank sheet of paper between the pages when coloring.

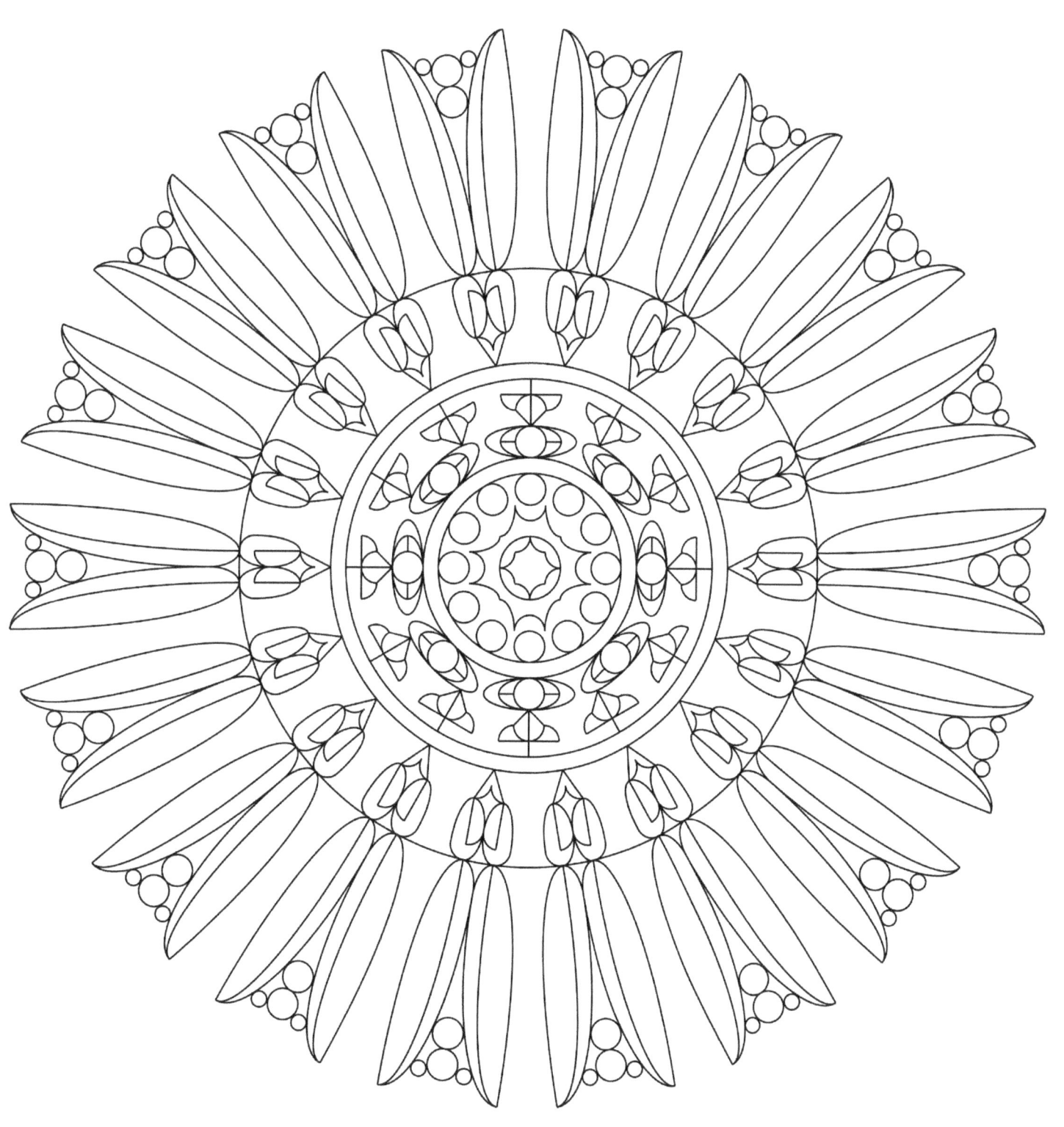

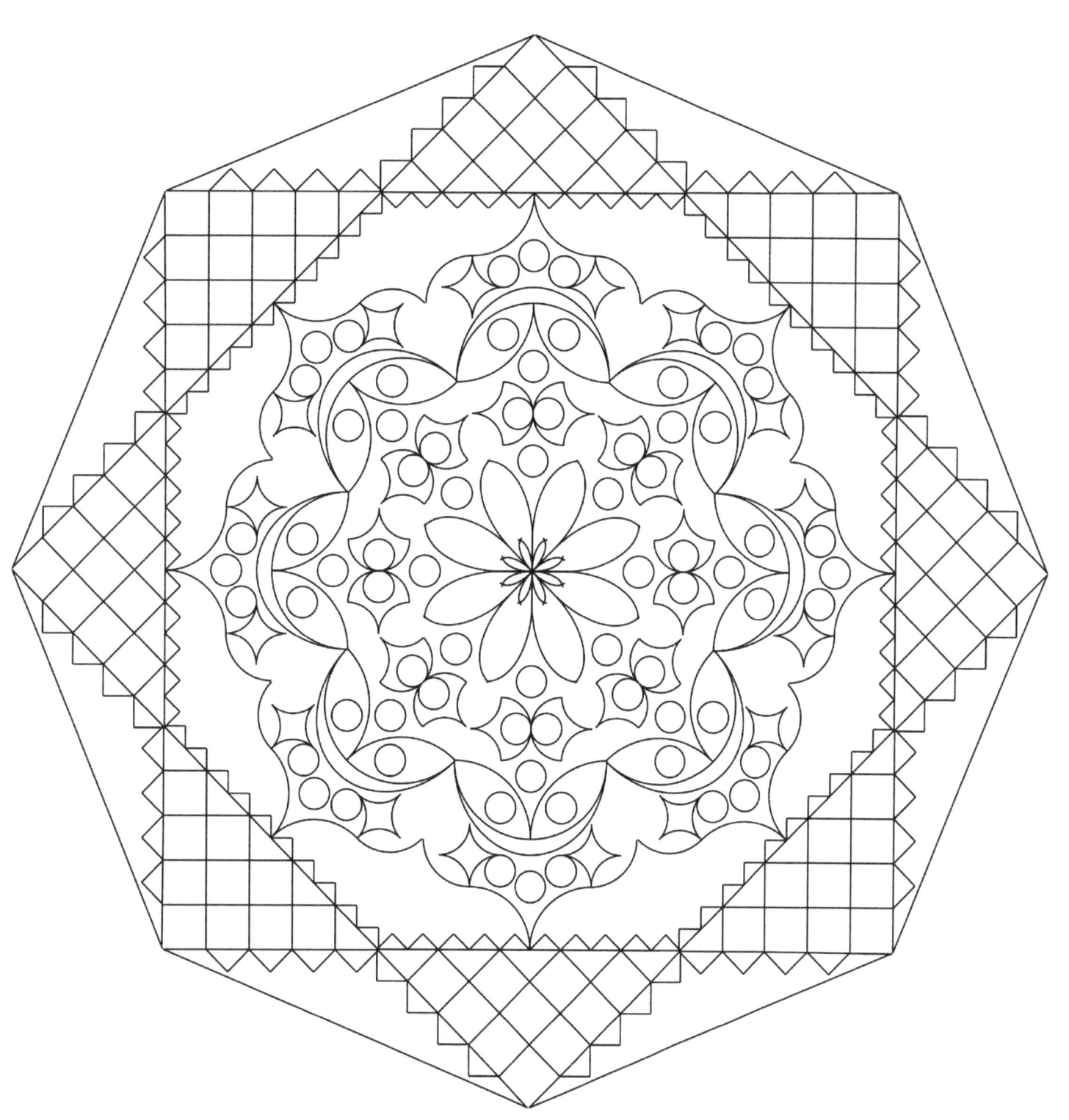

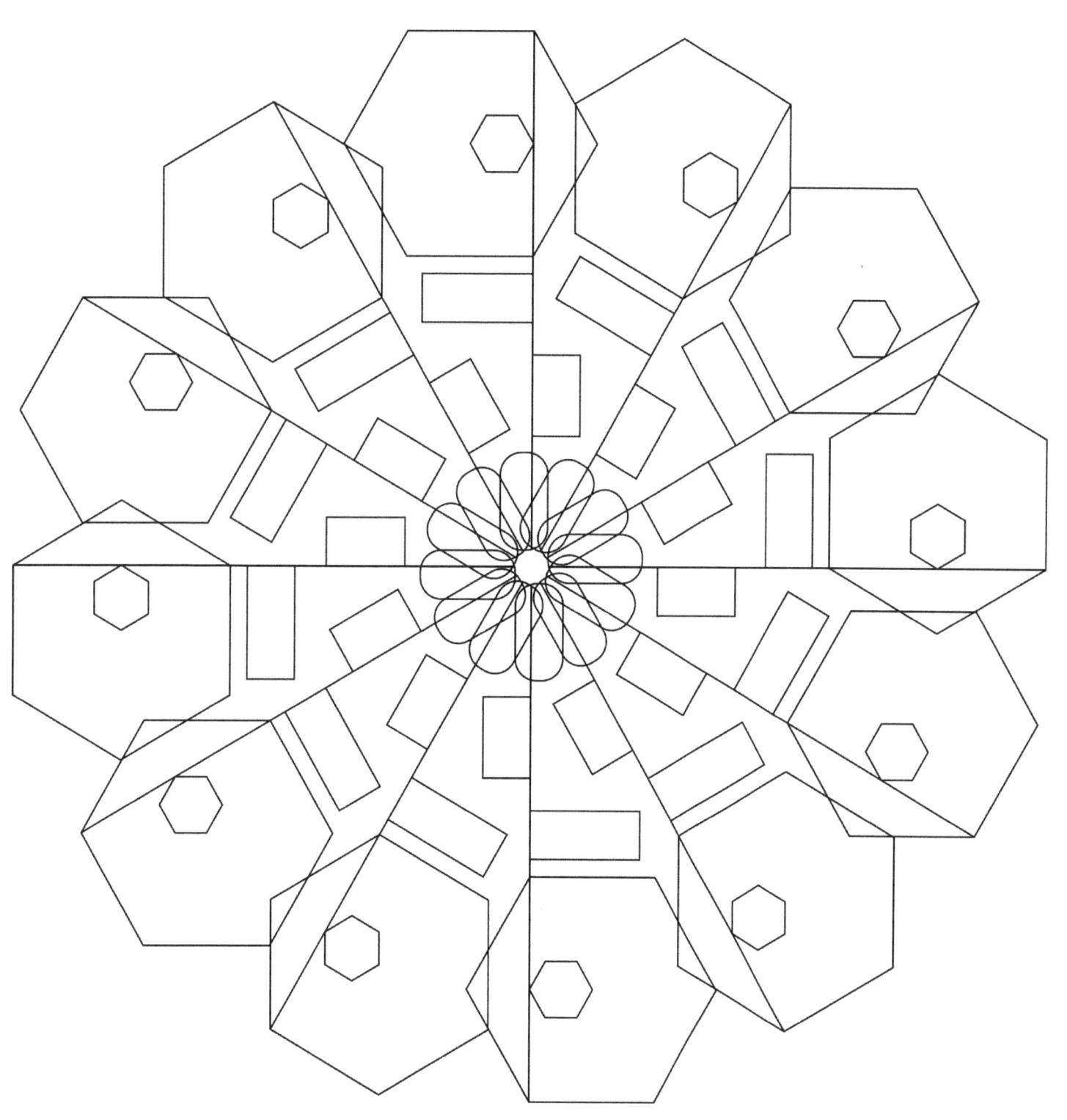

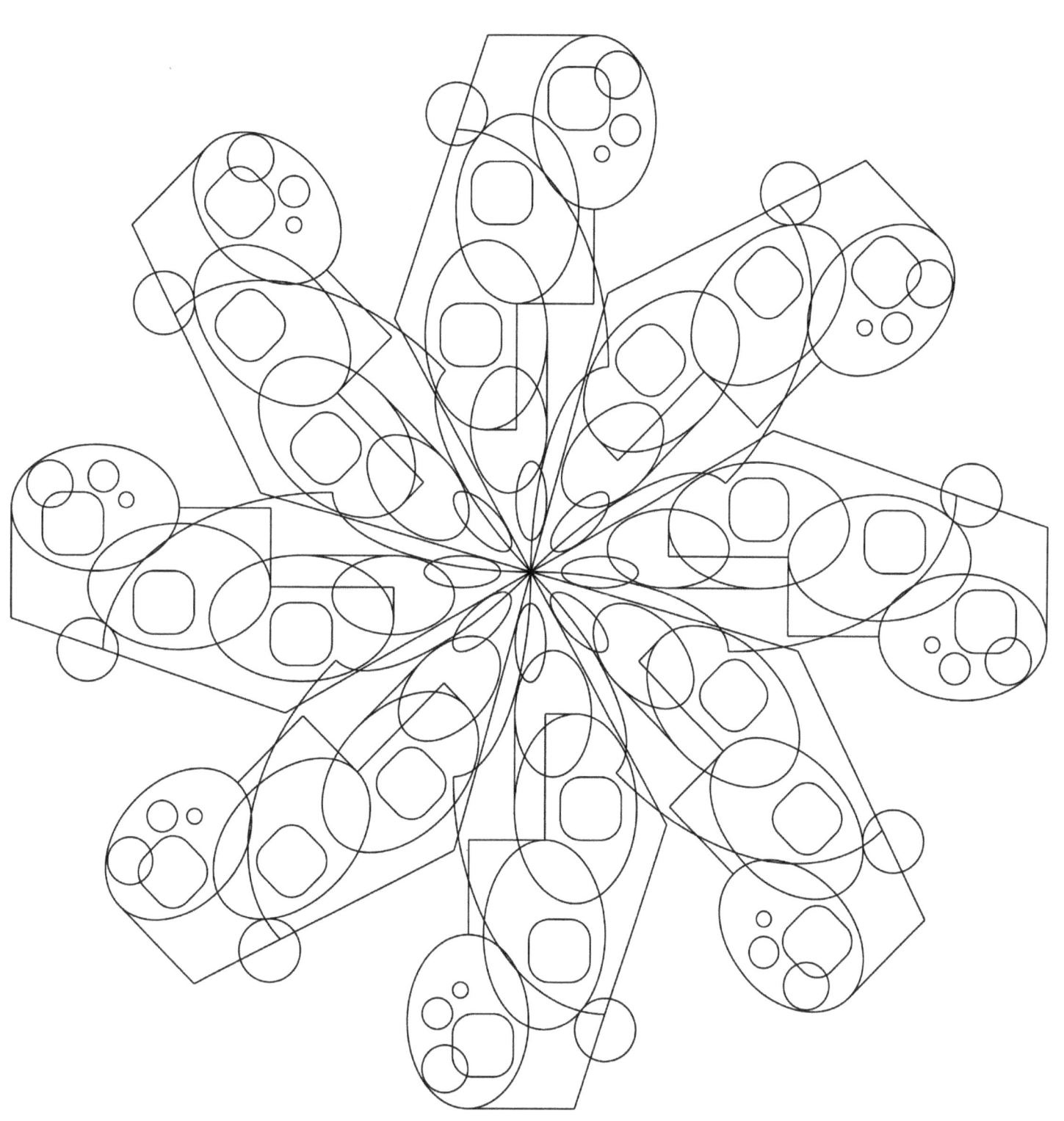

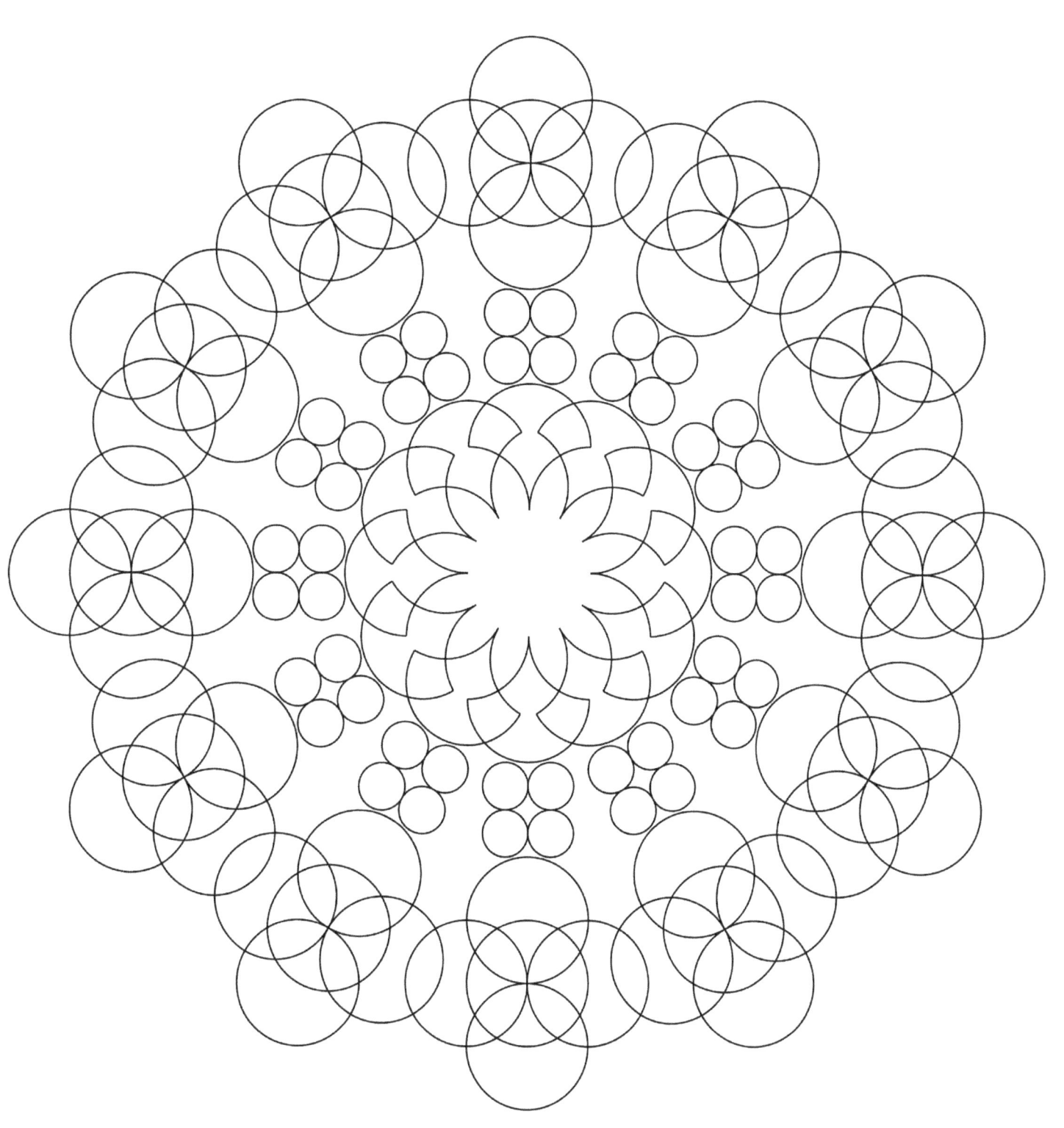

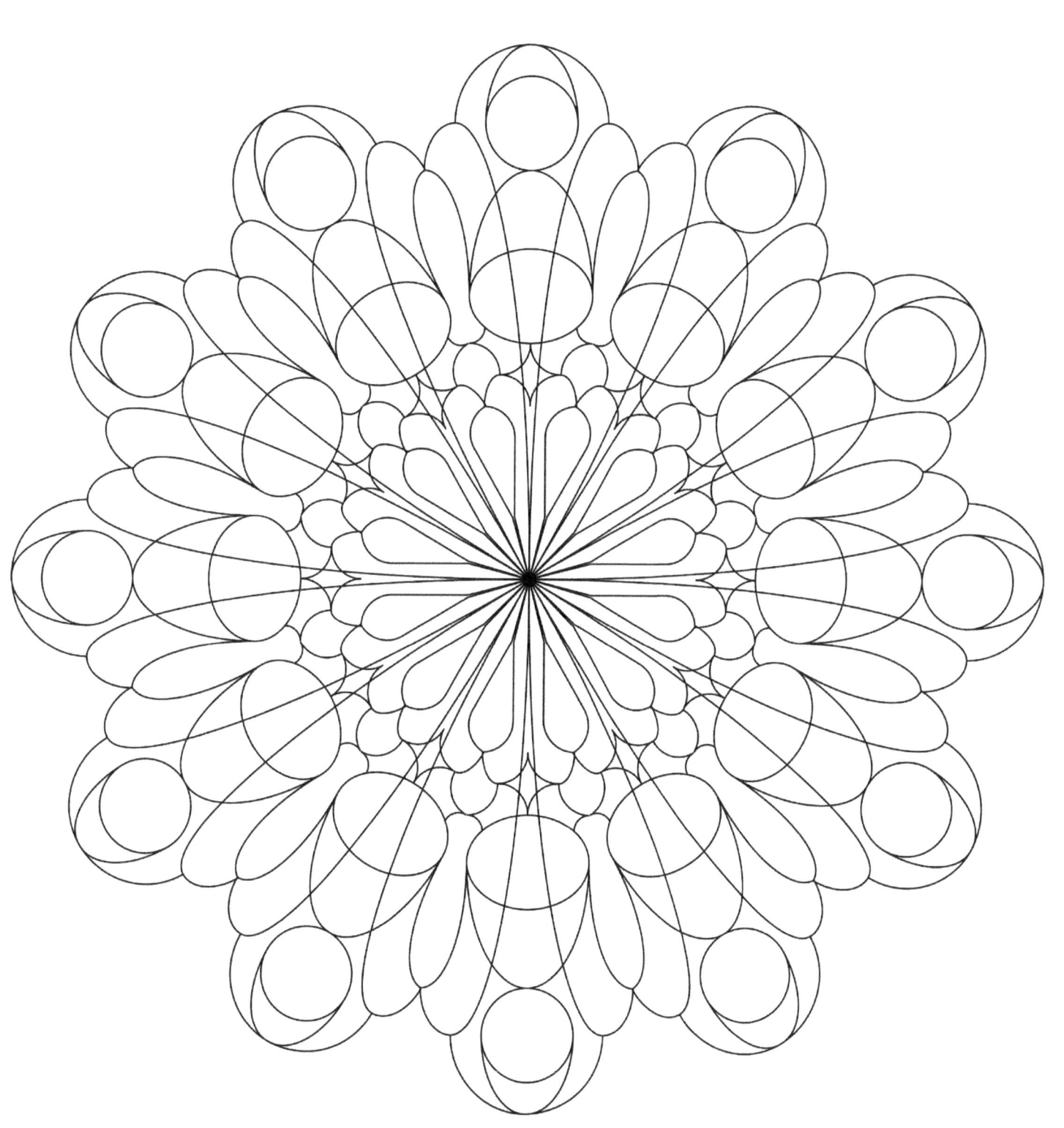

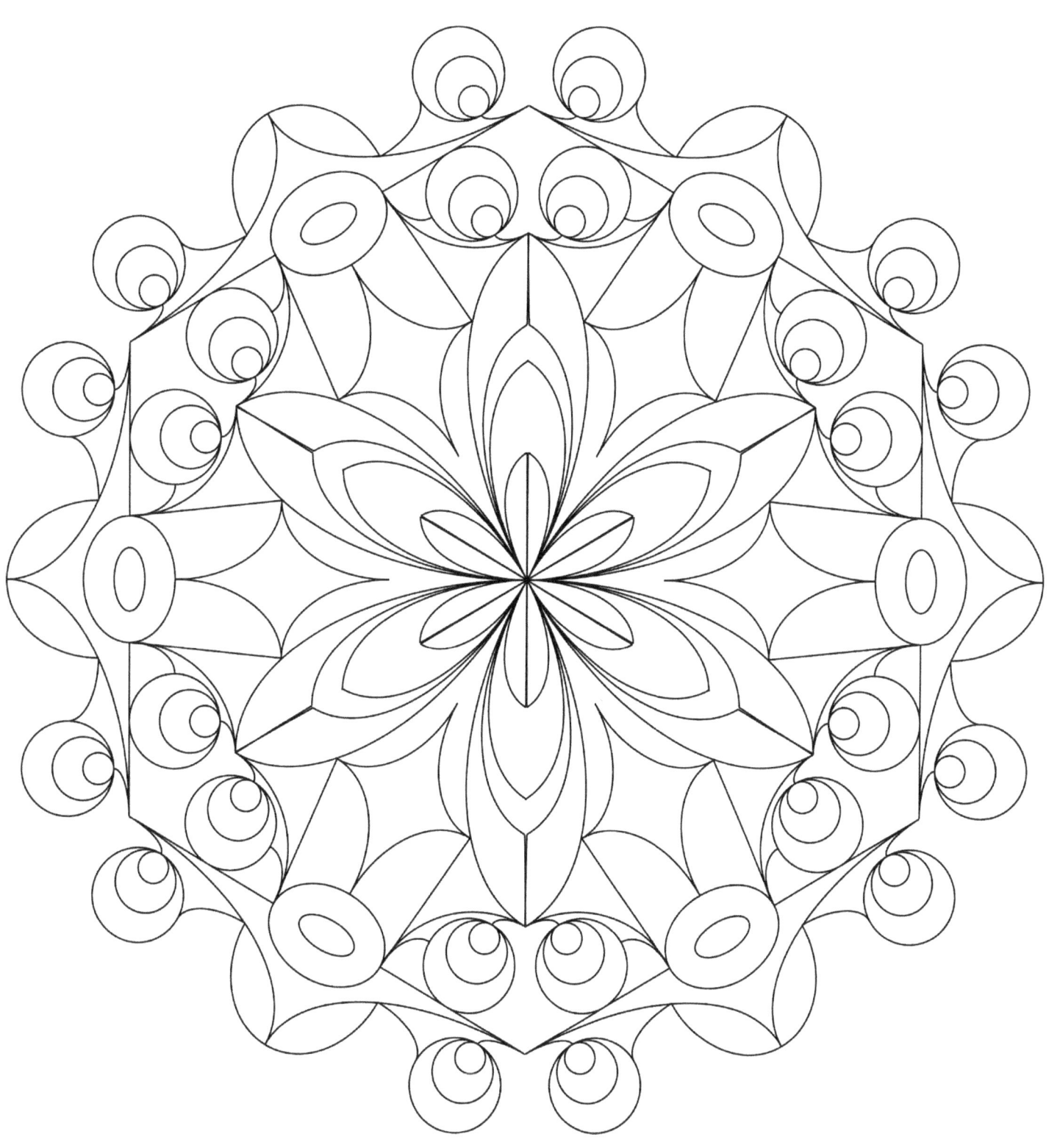

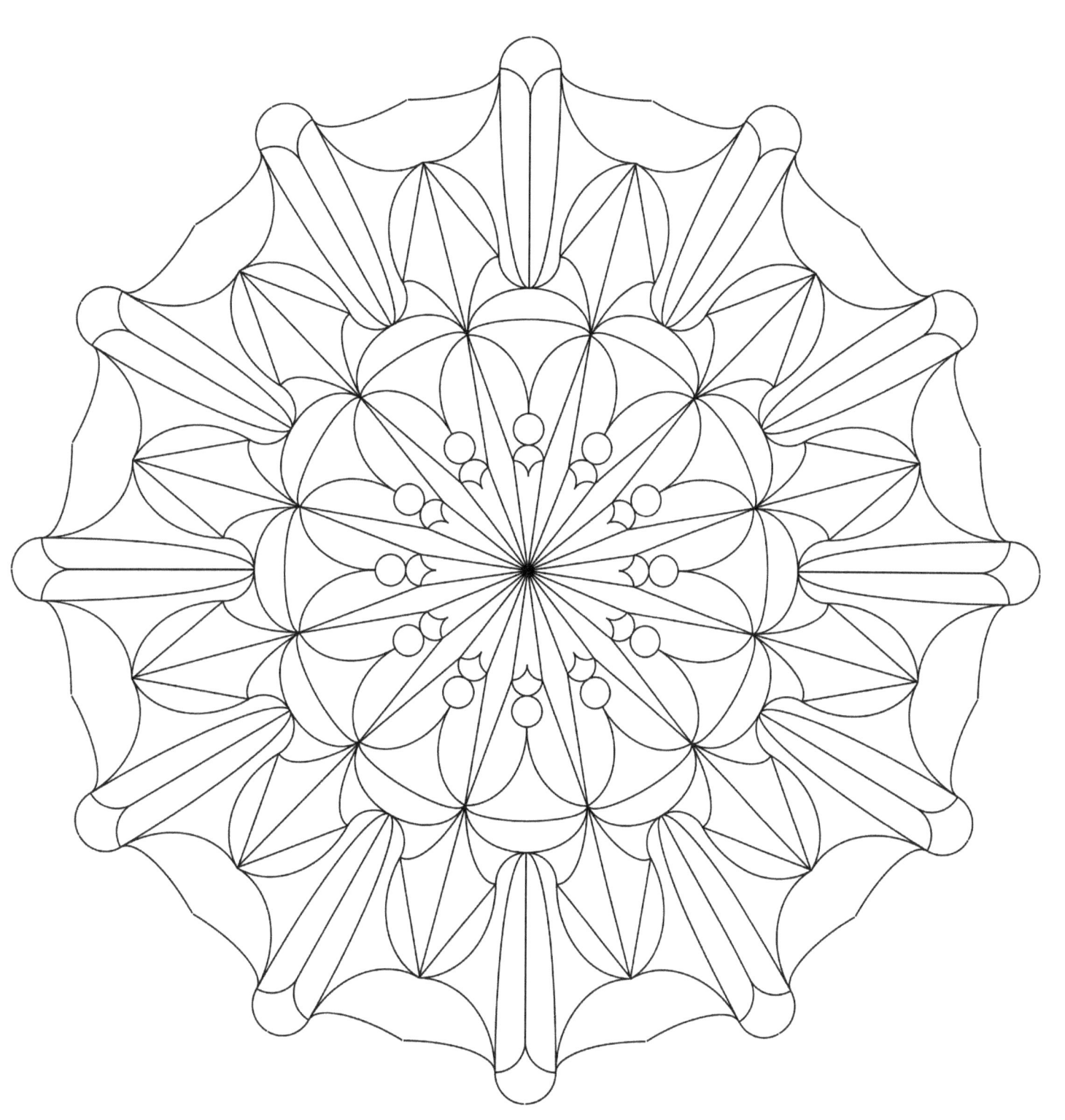

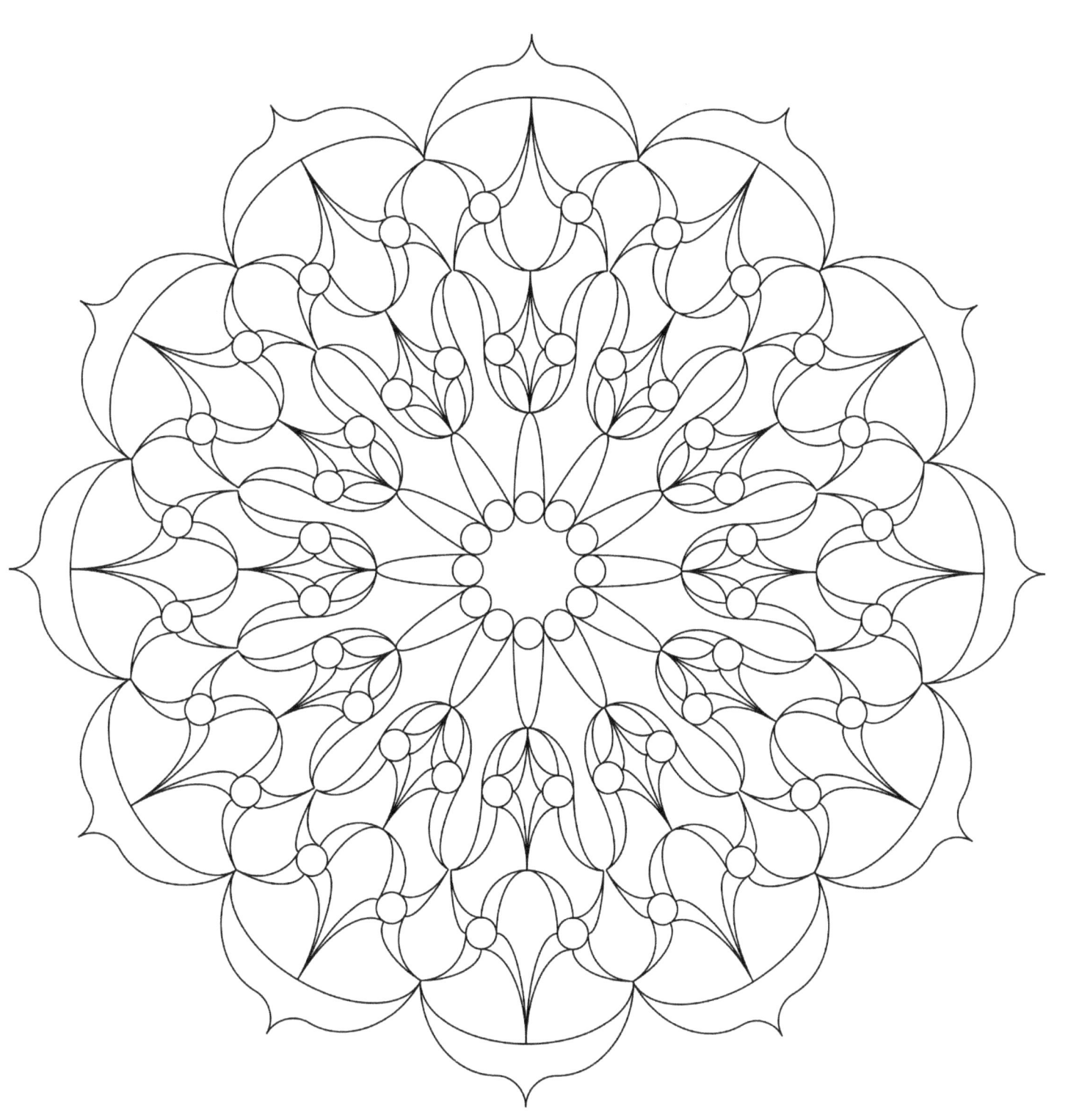

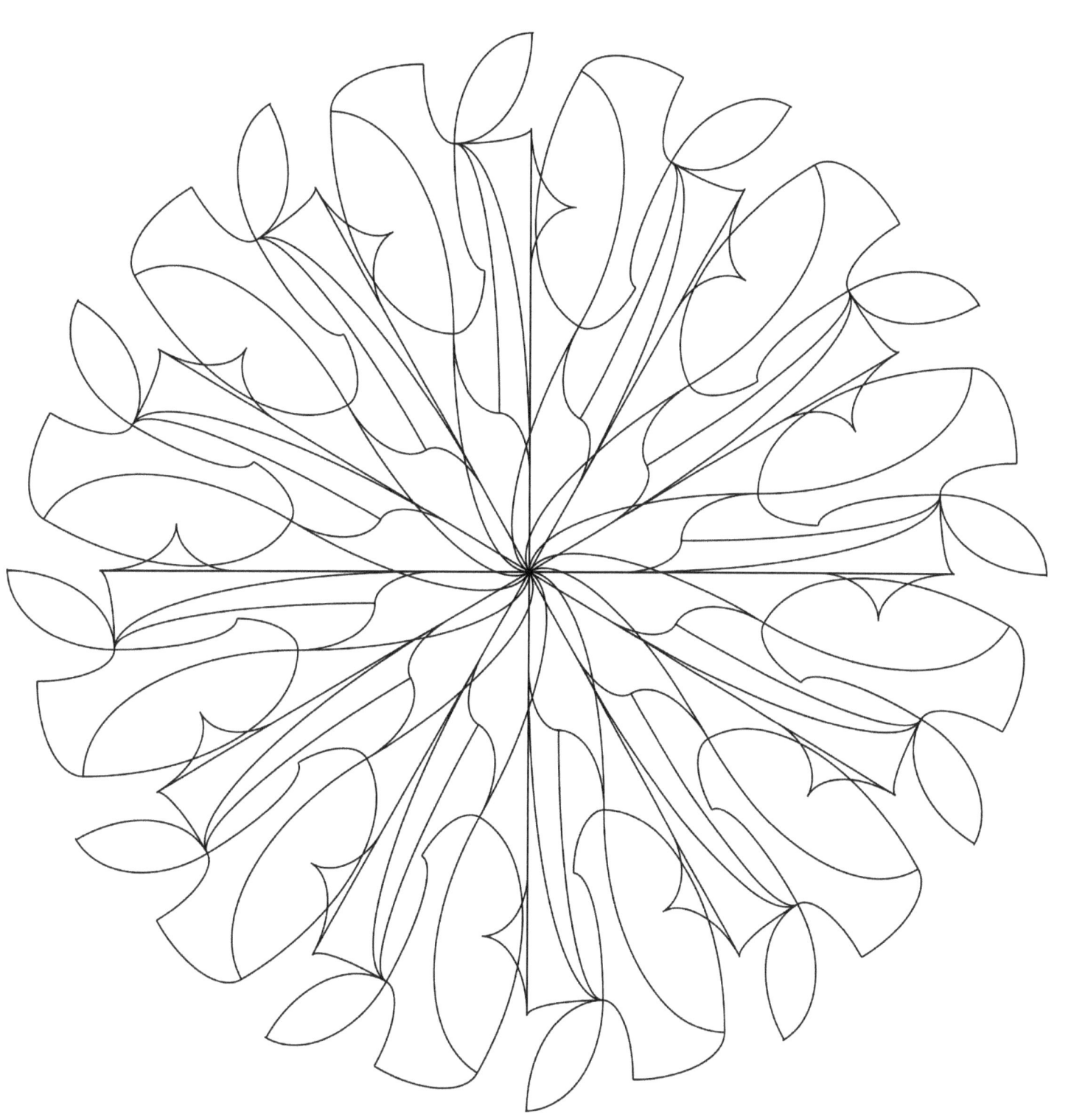

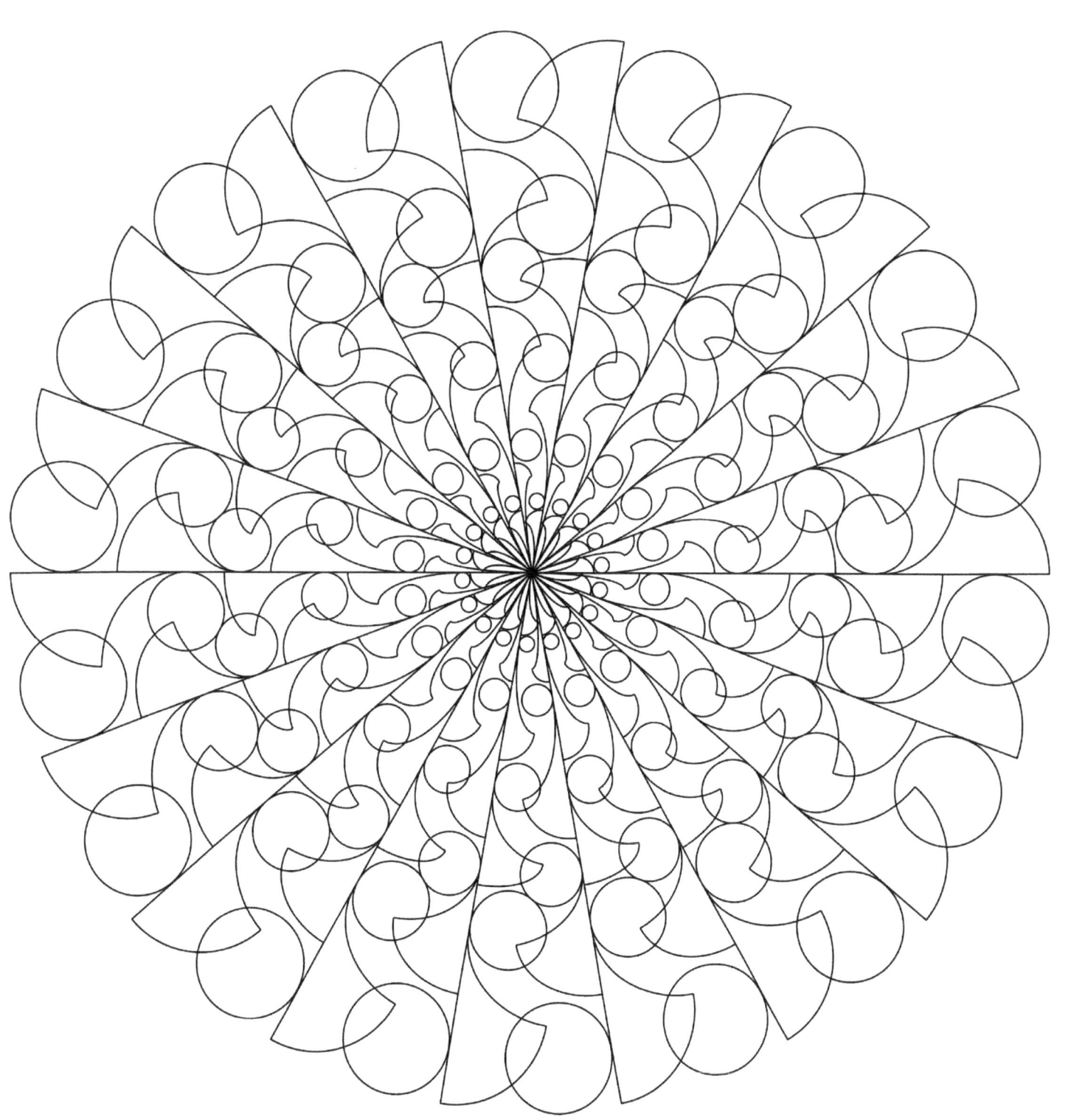

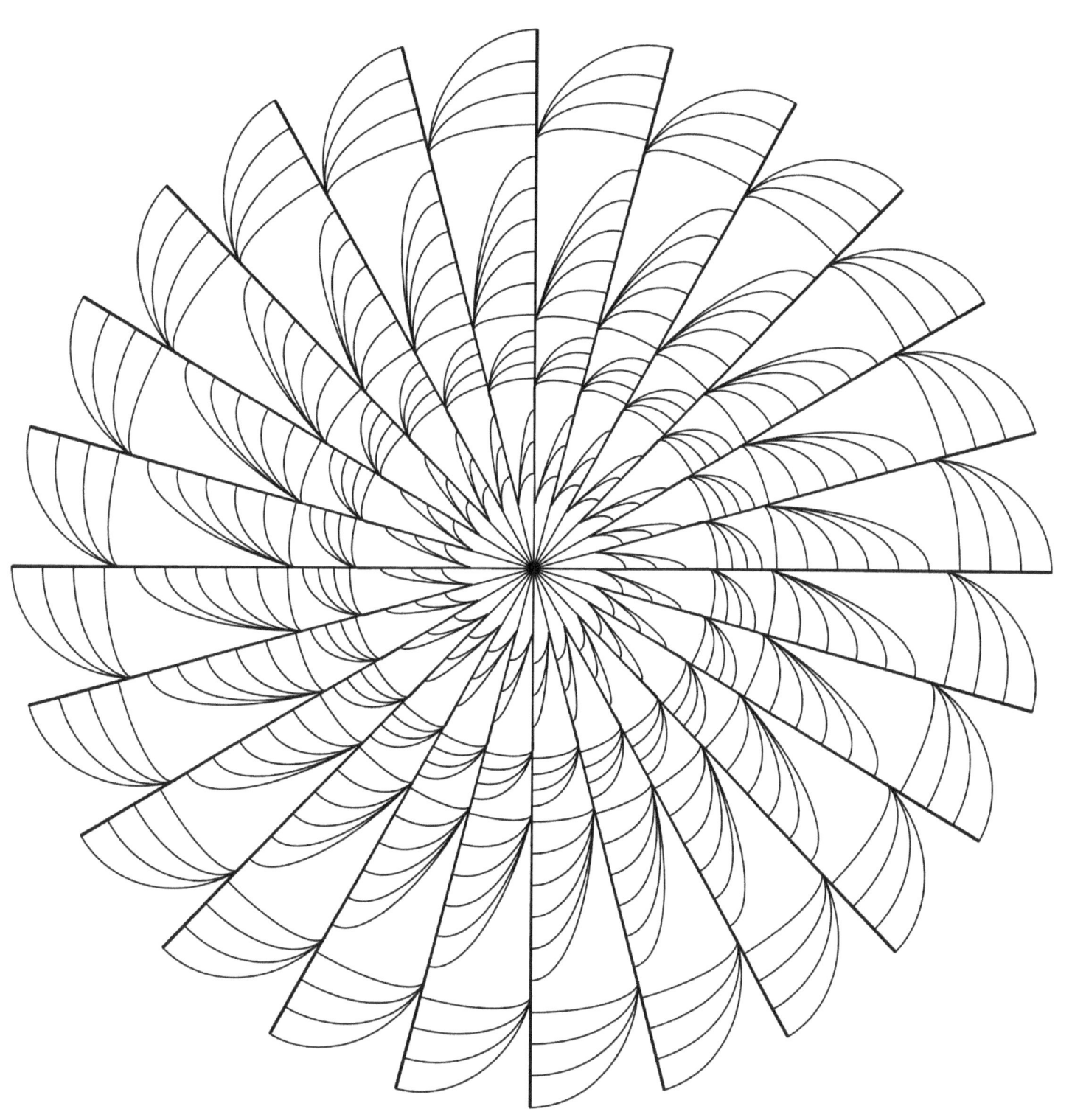

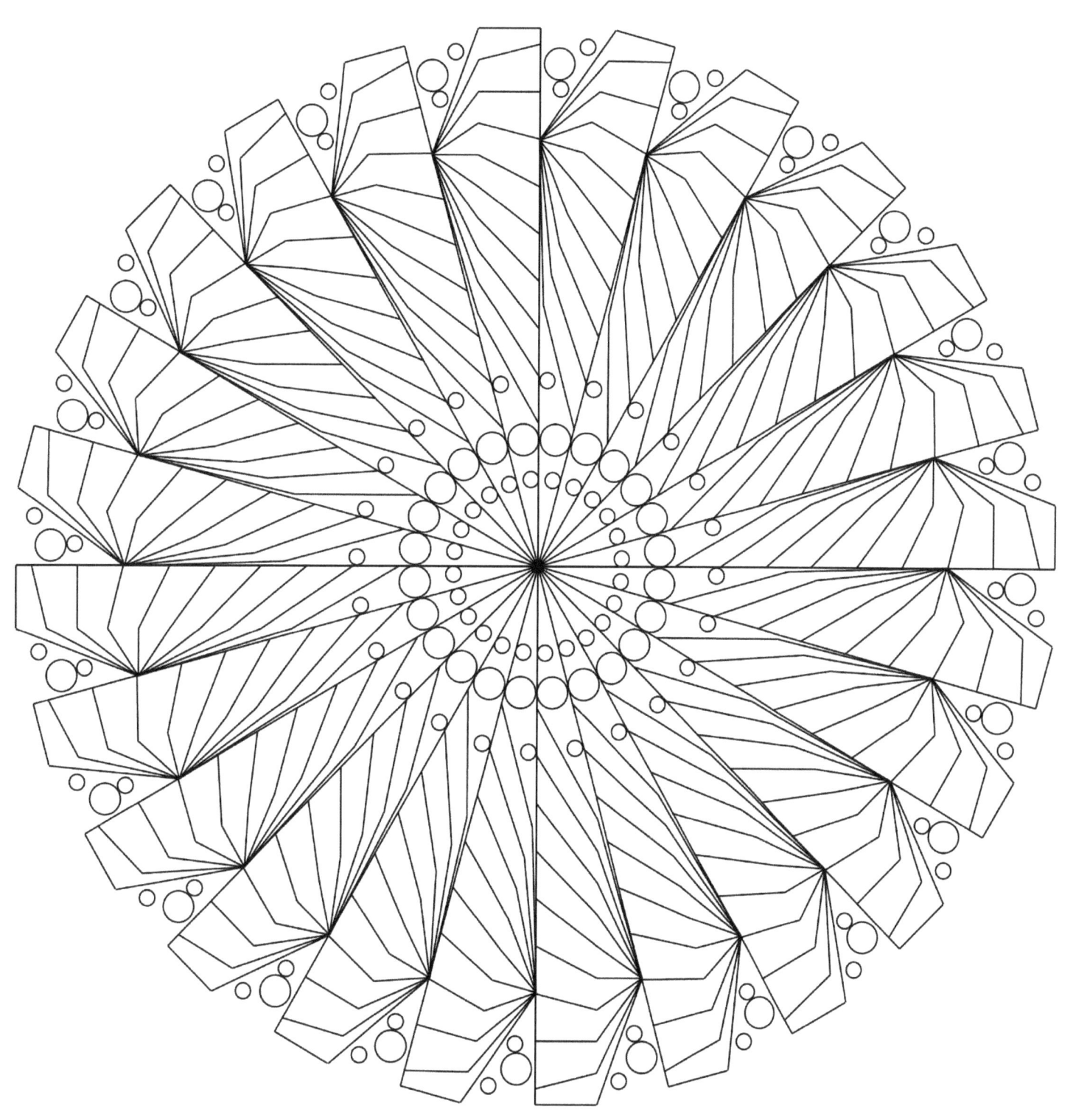

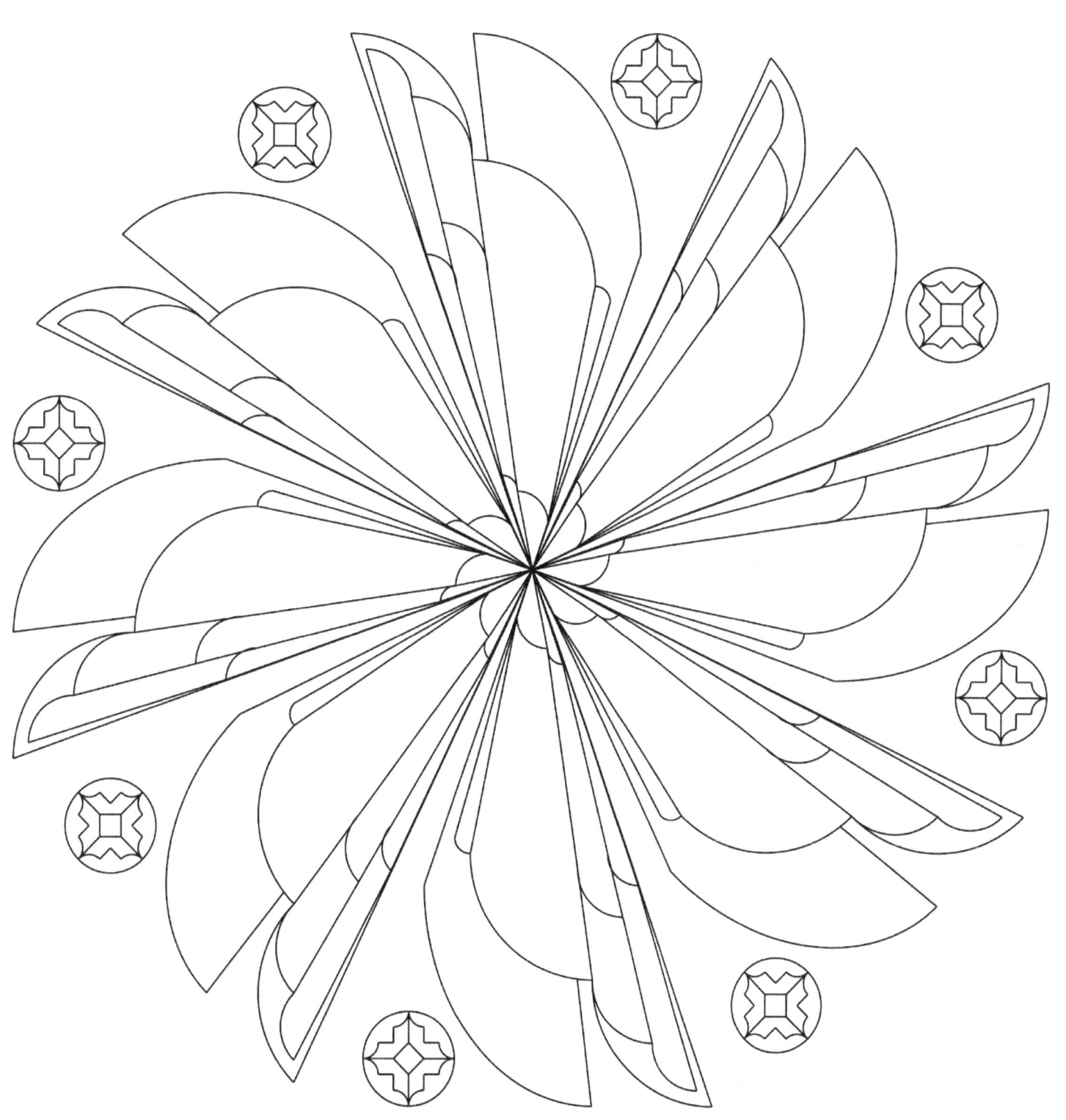

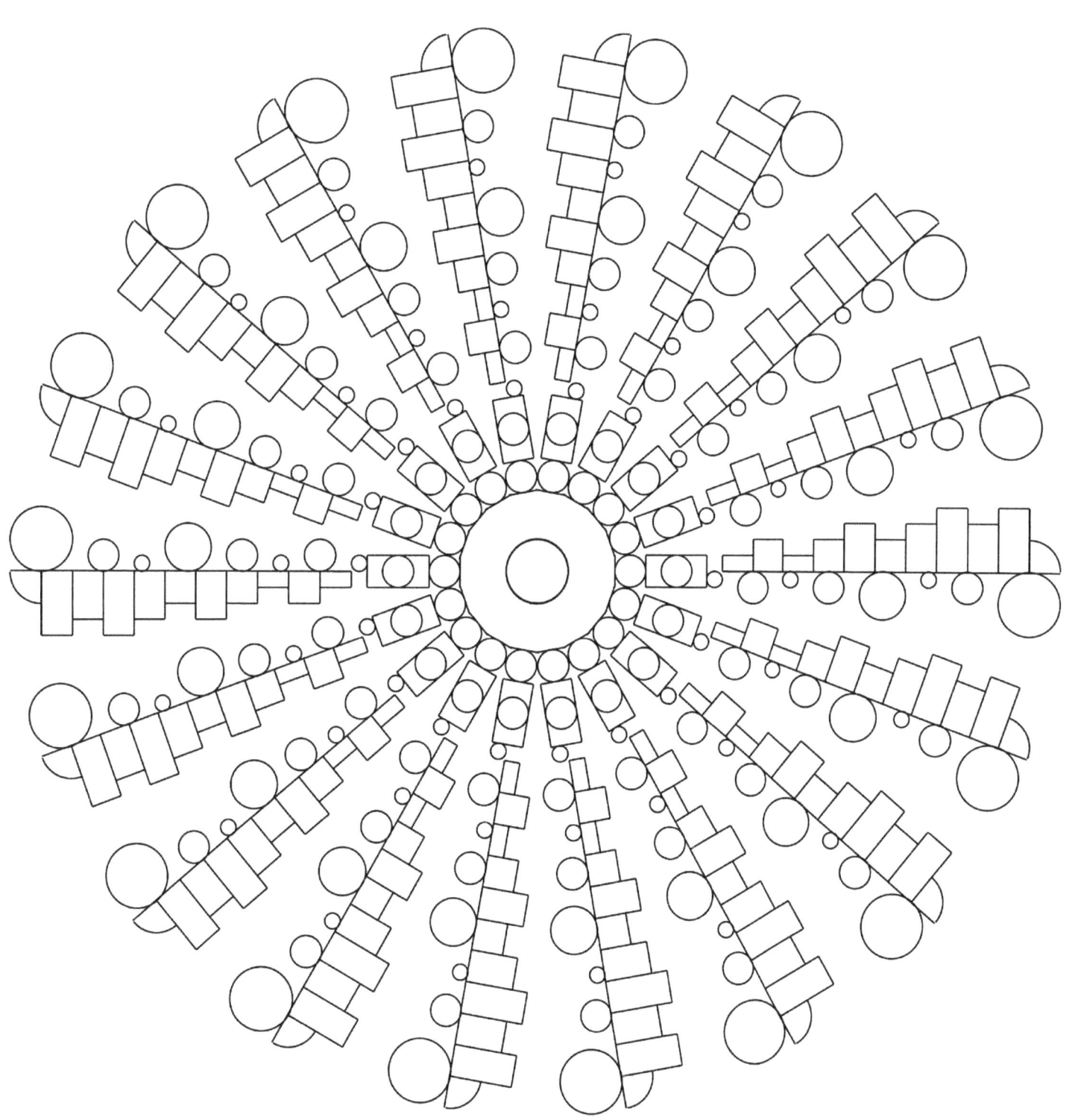

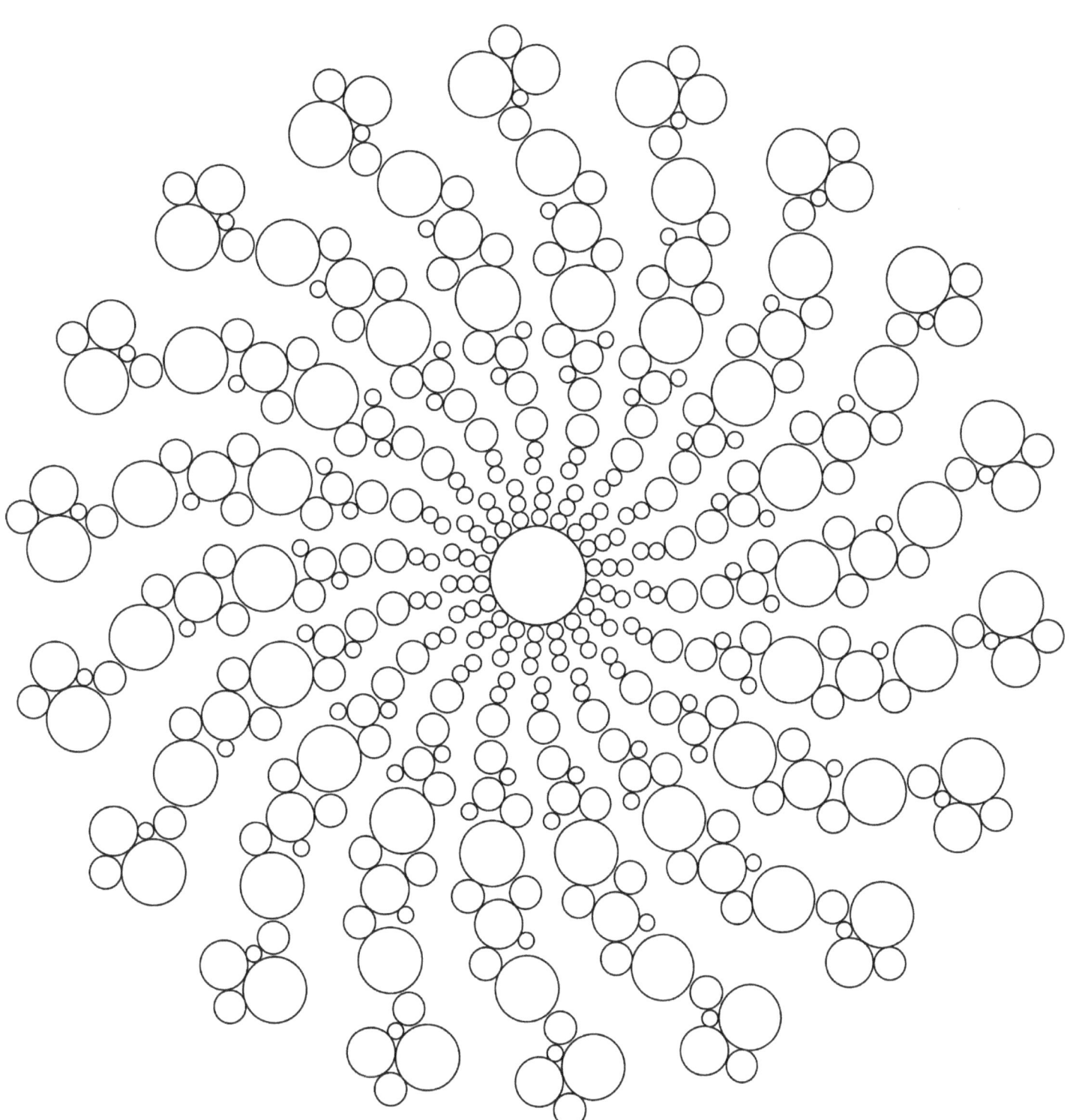

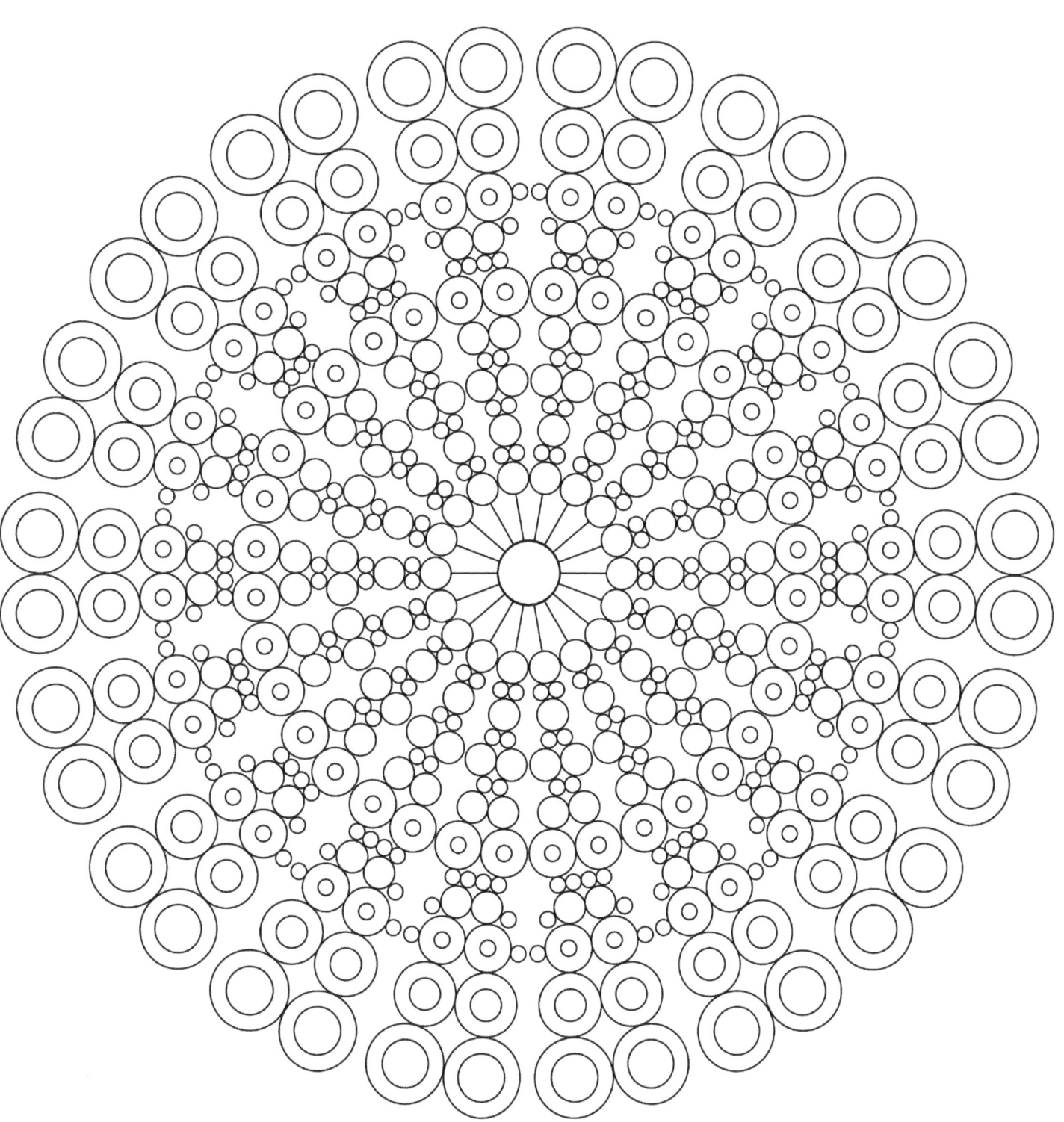

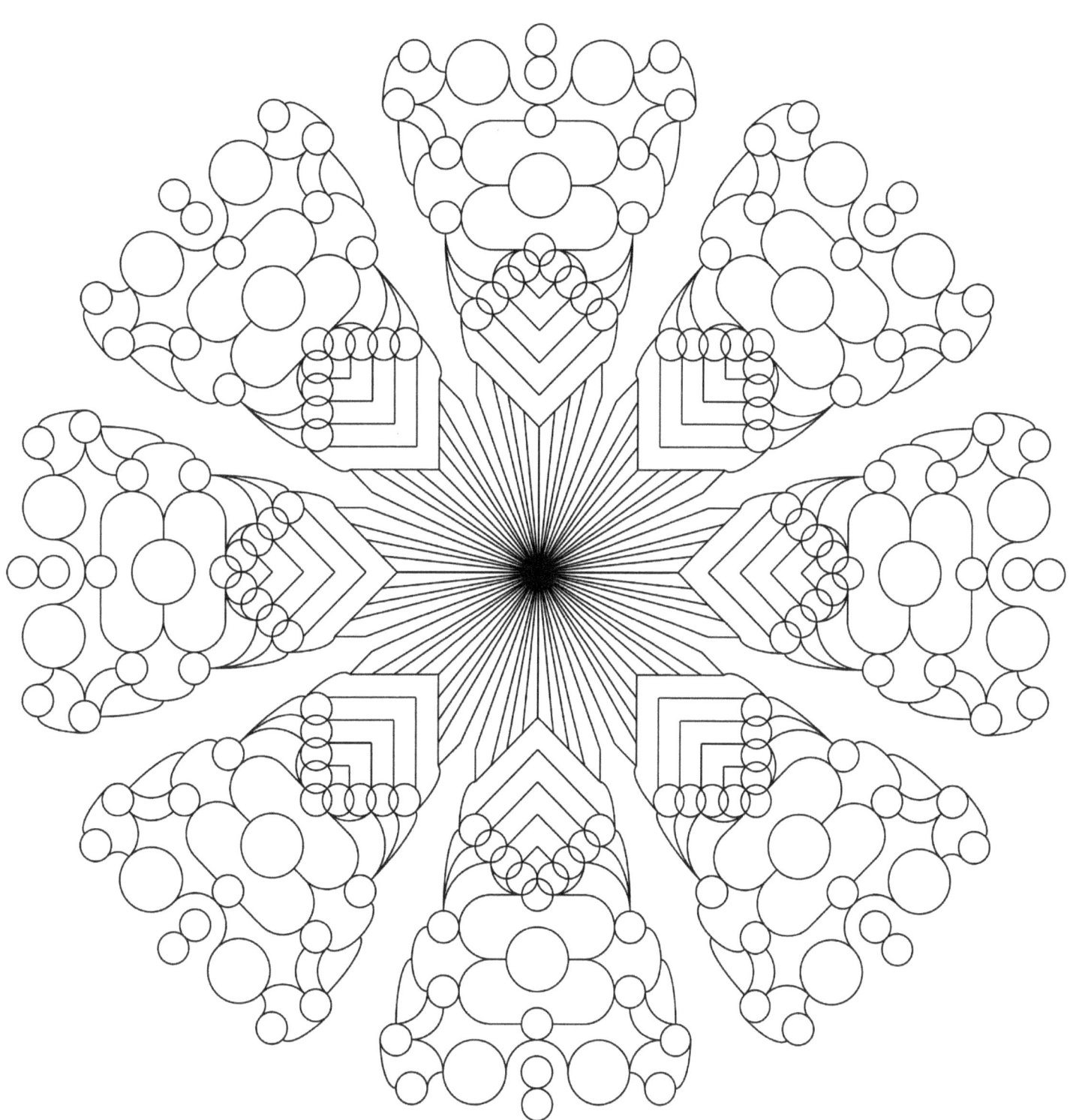

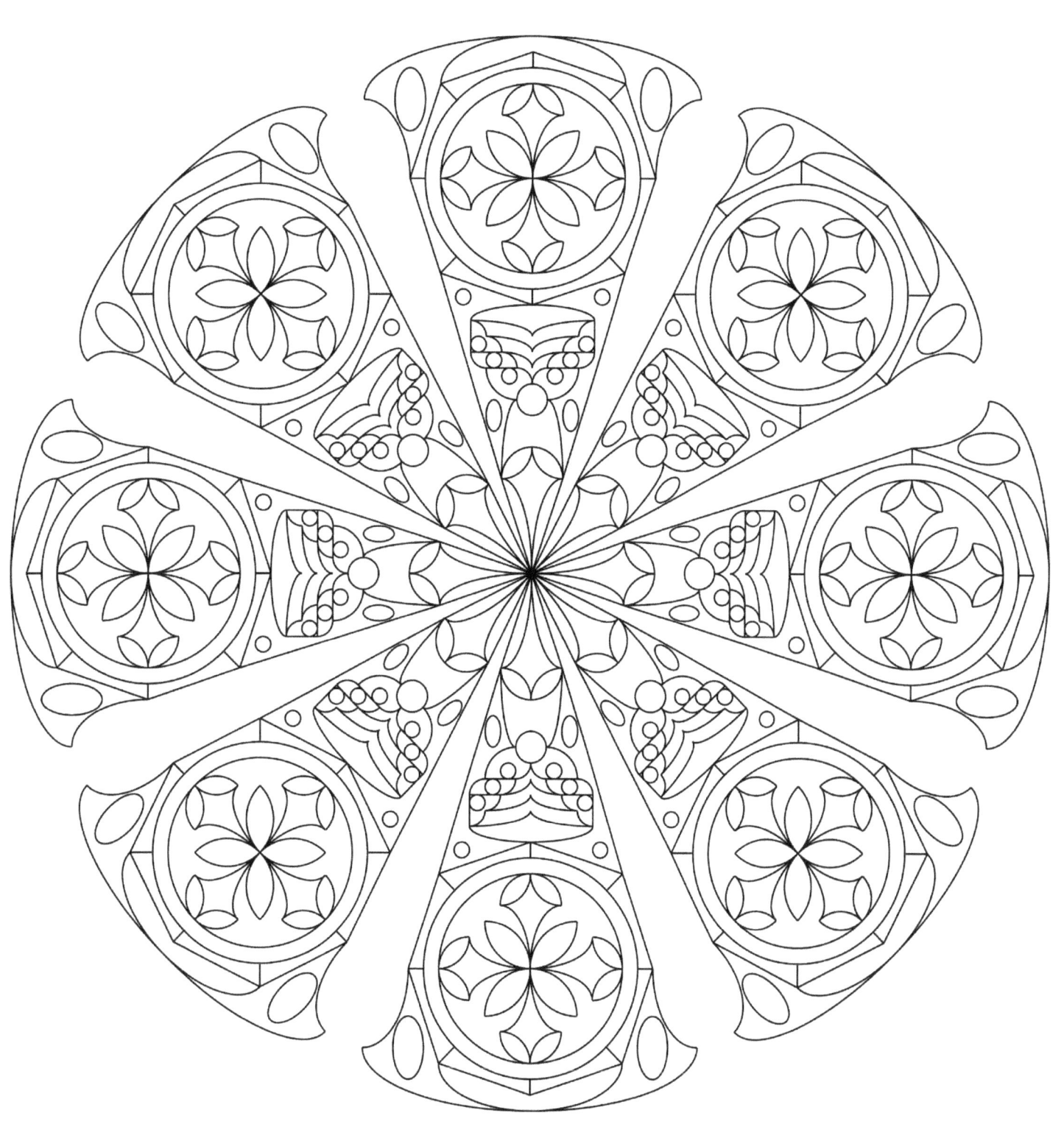

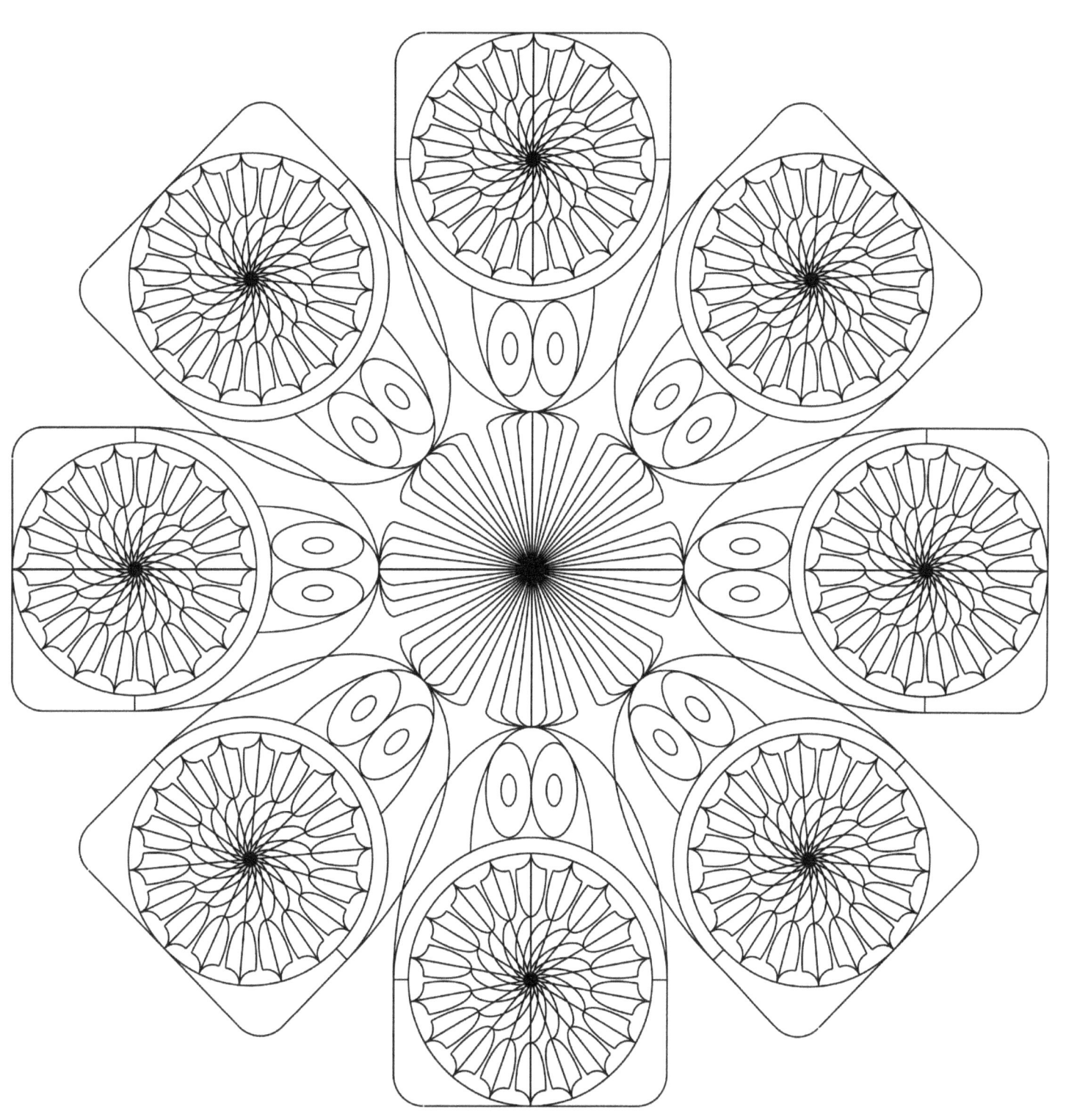

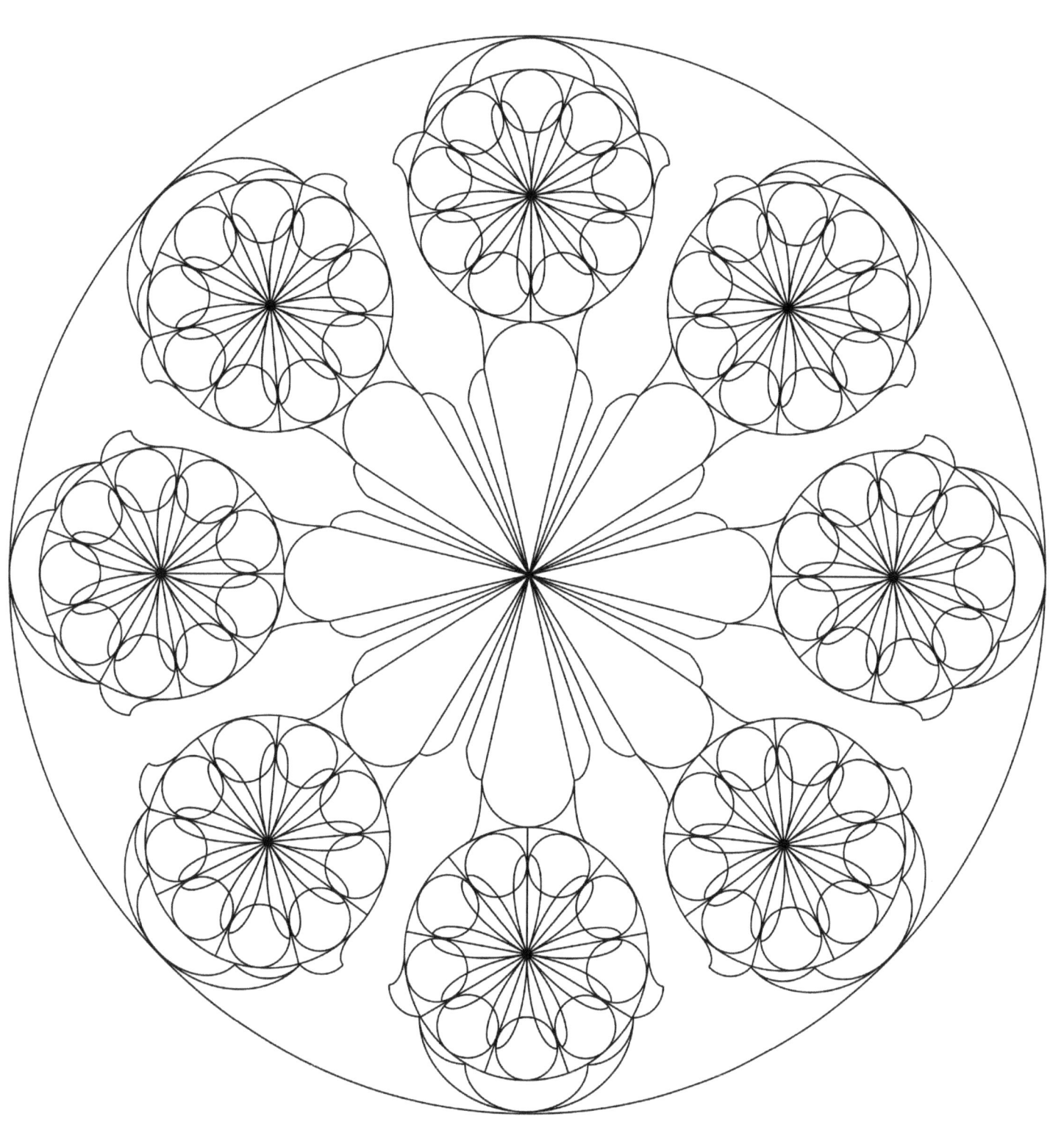

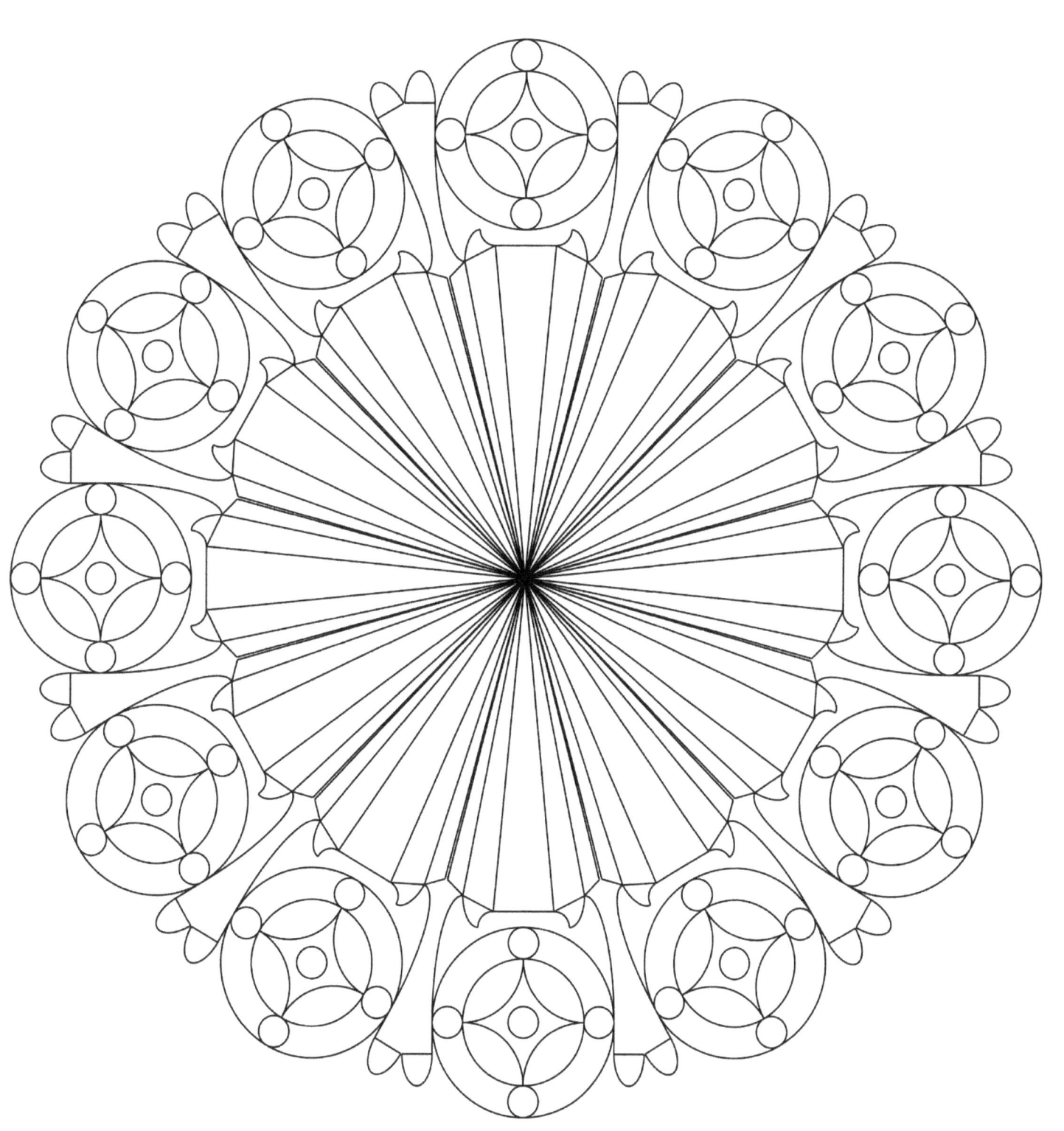

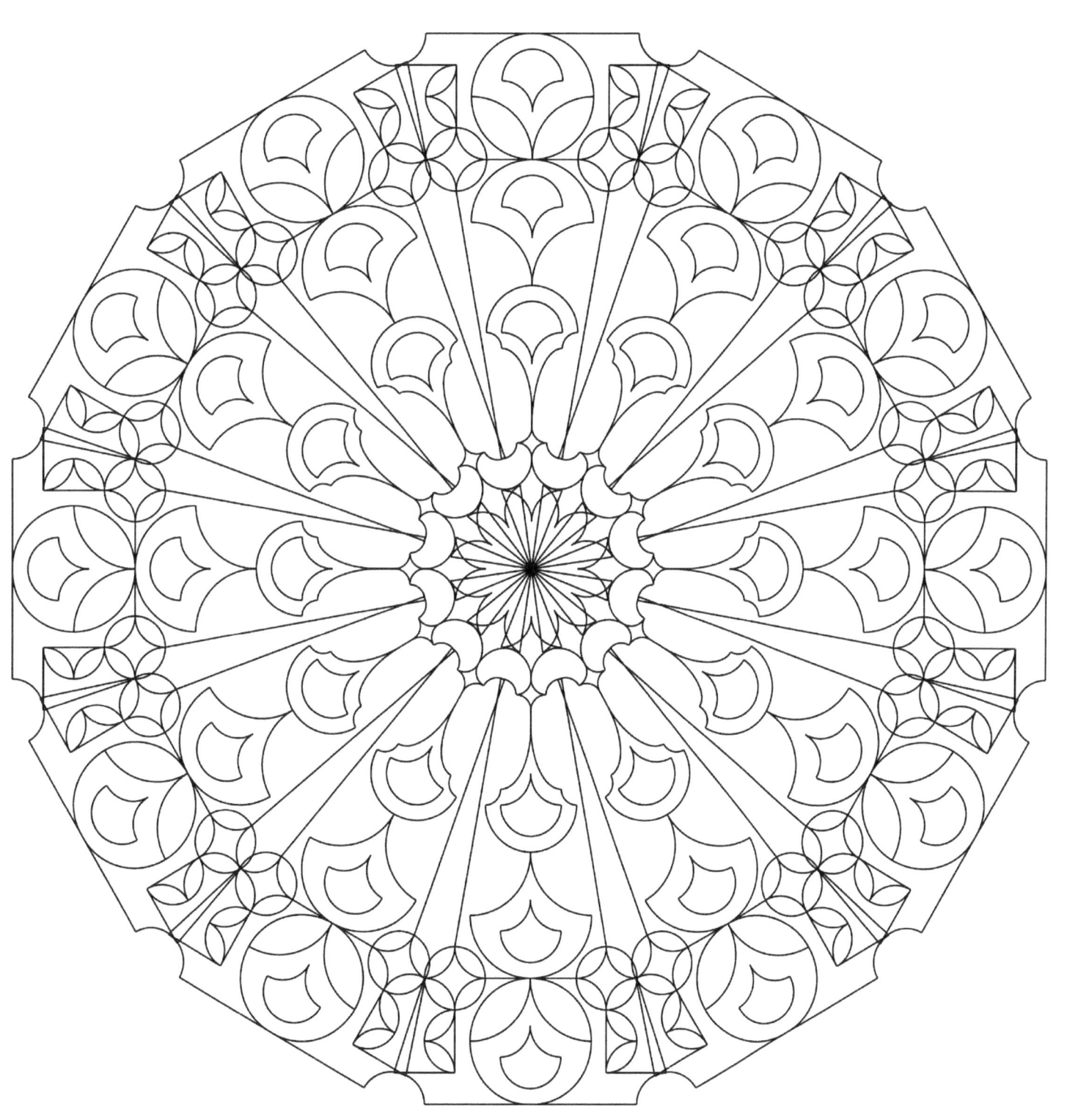

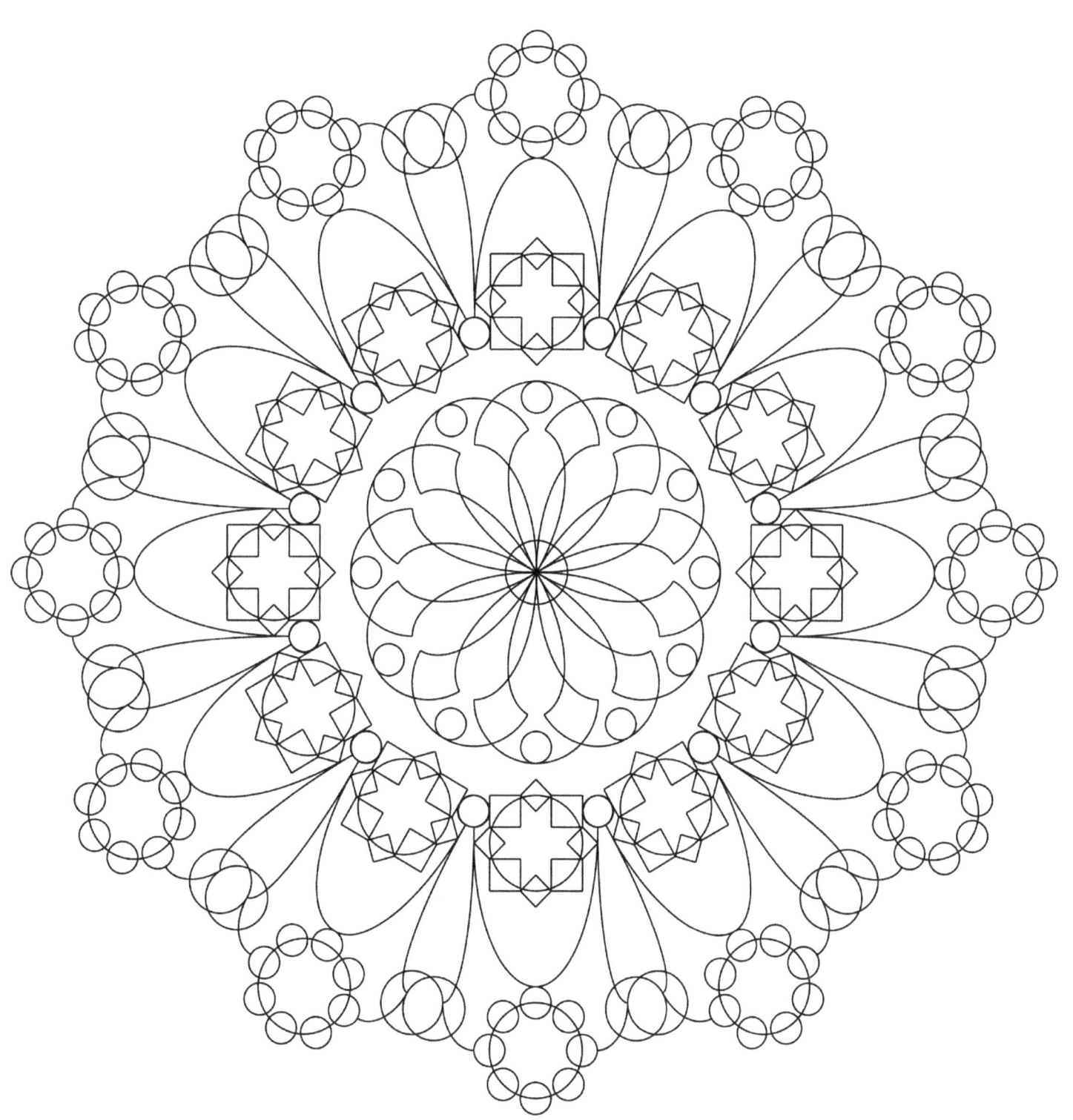

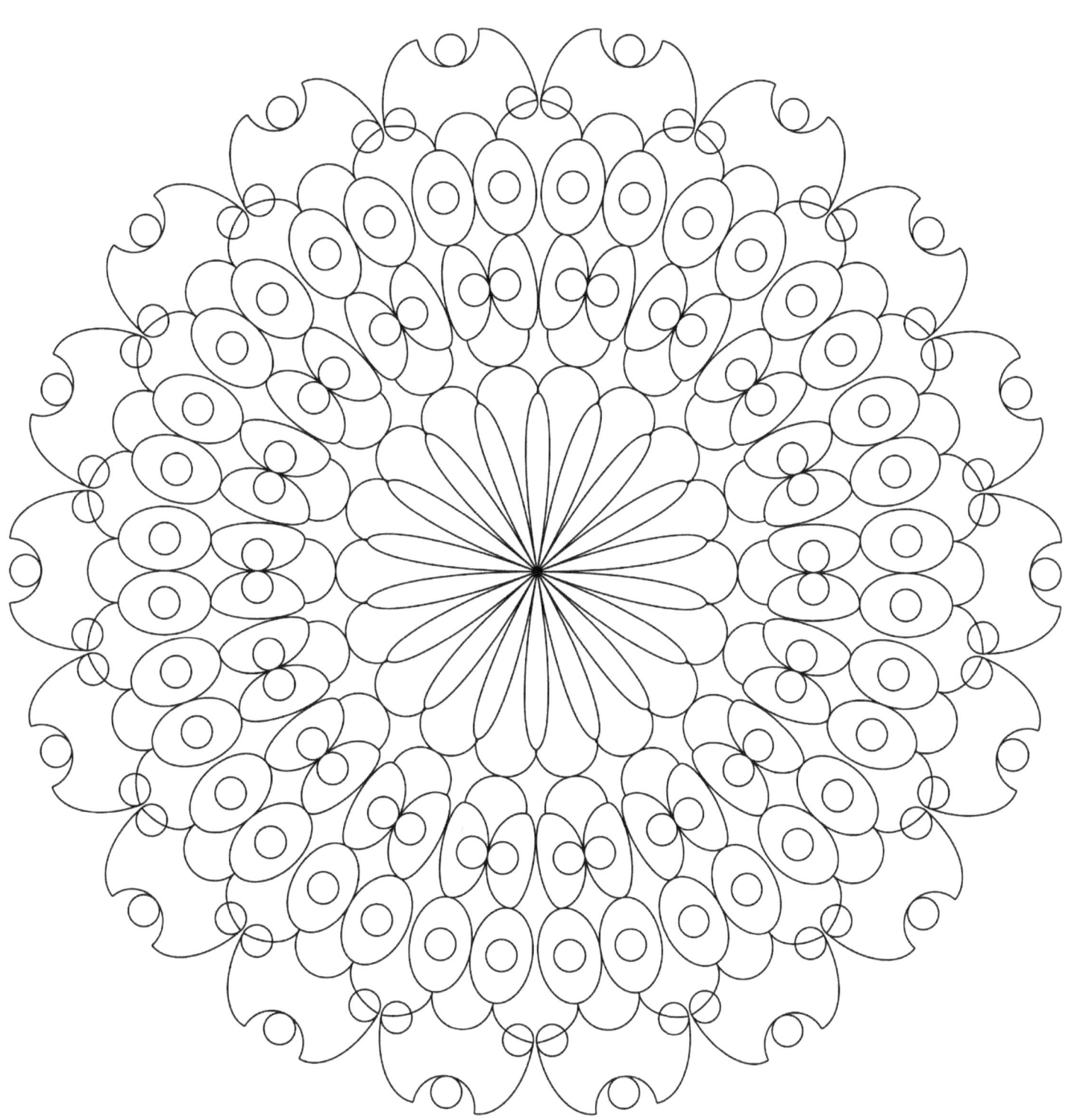

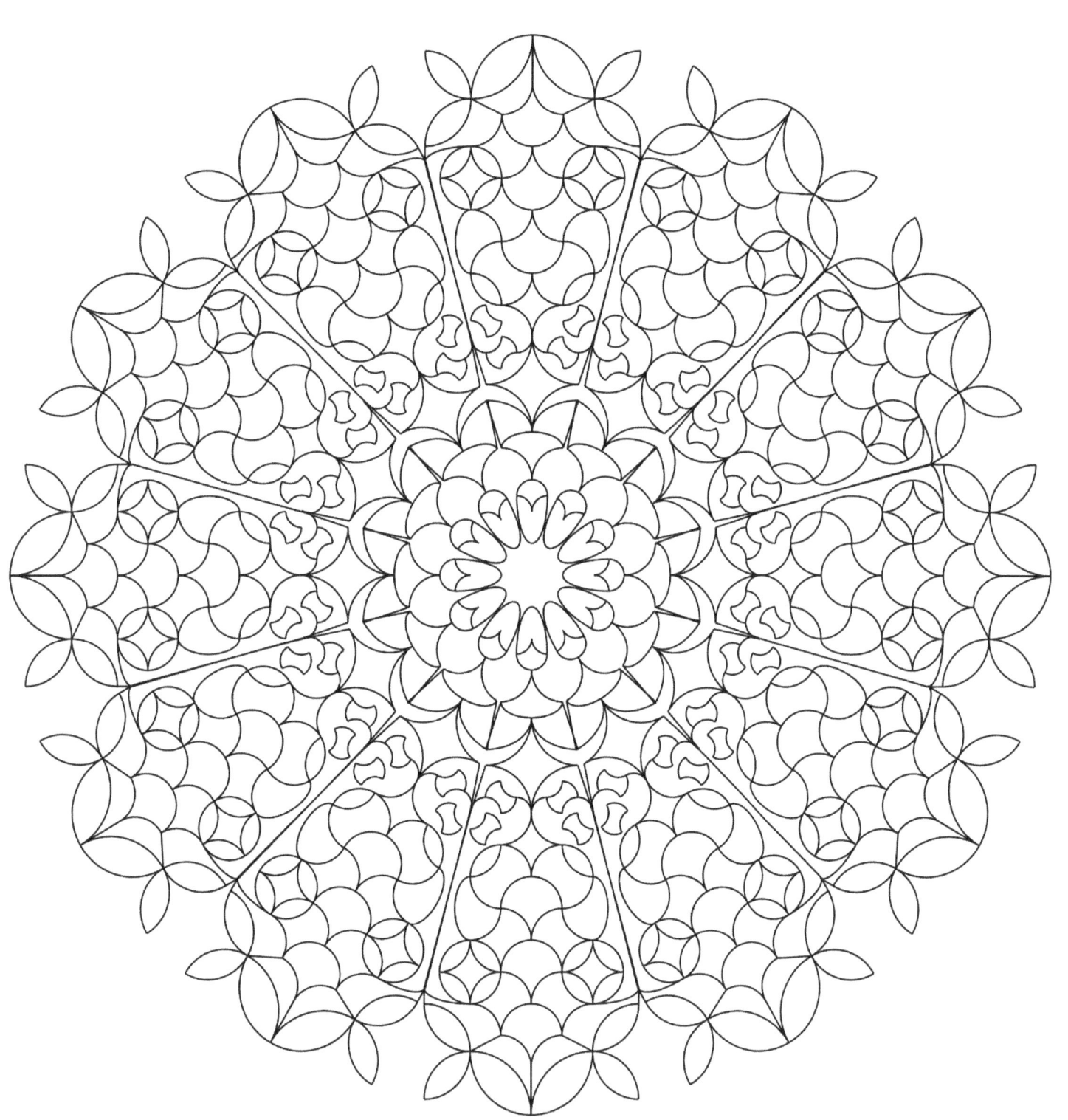

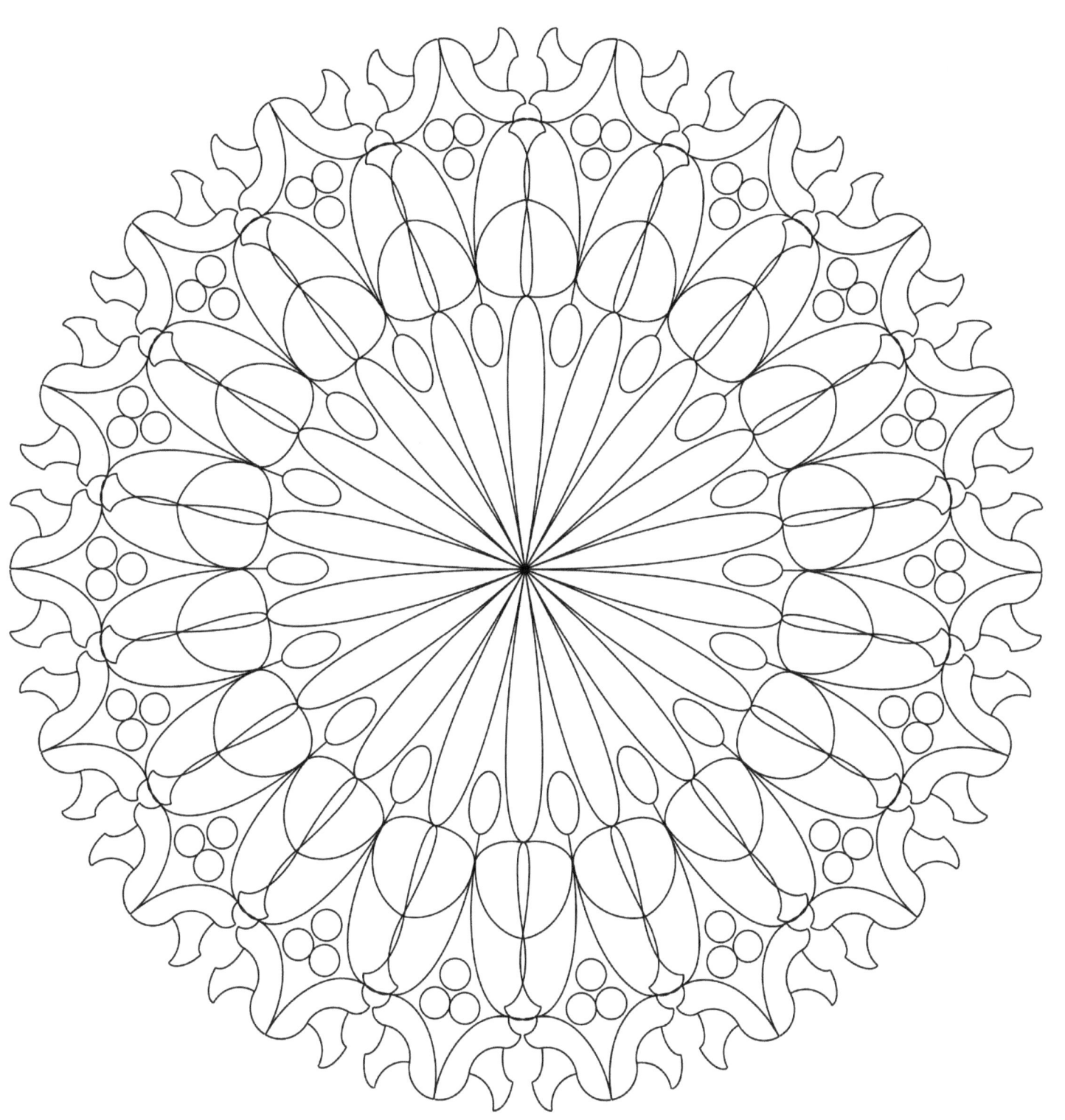

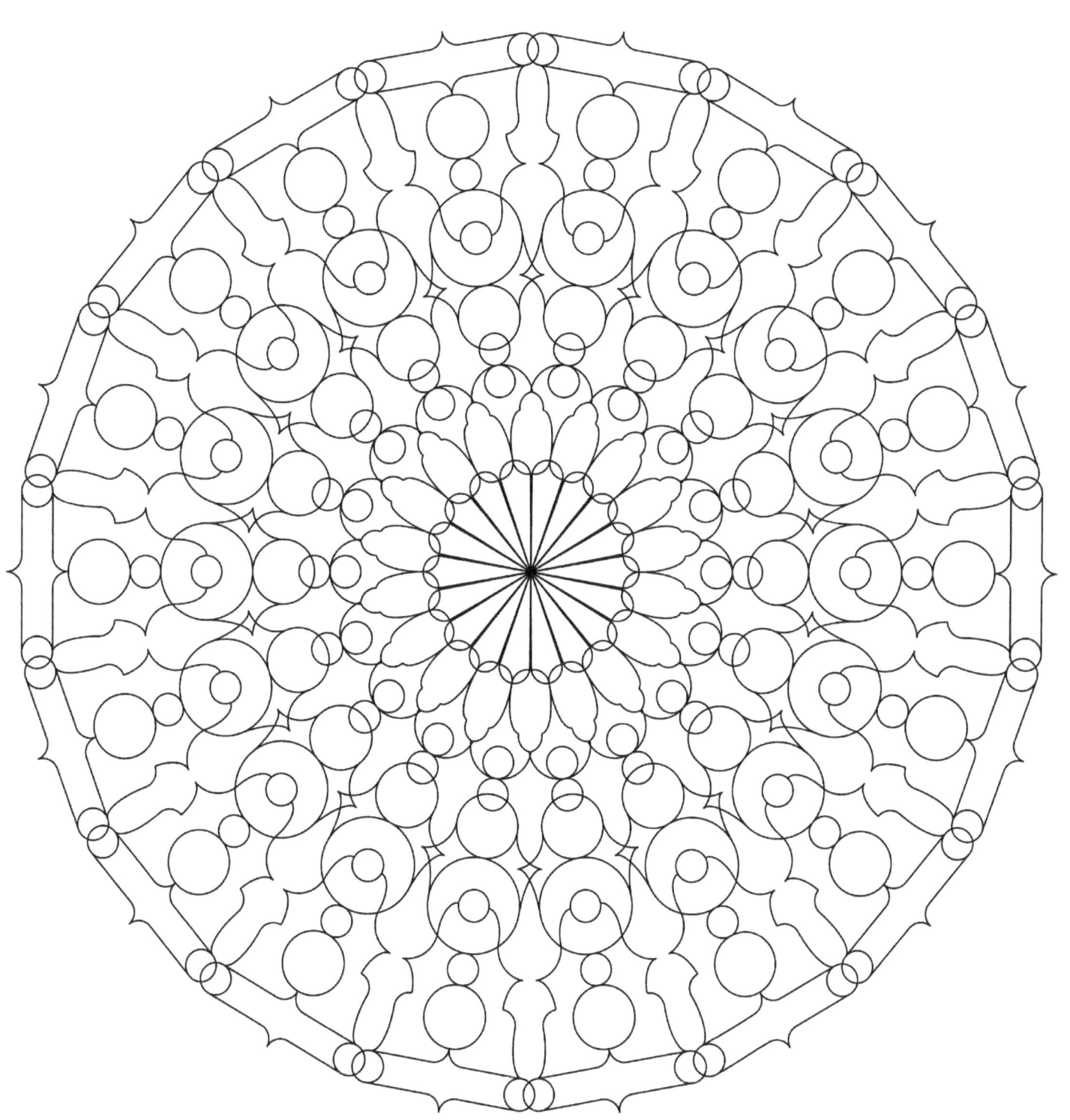

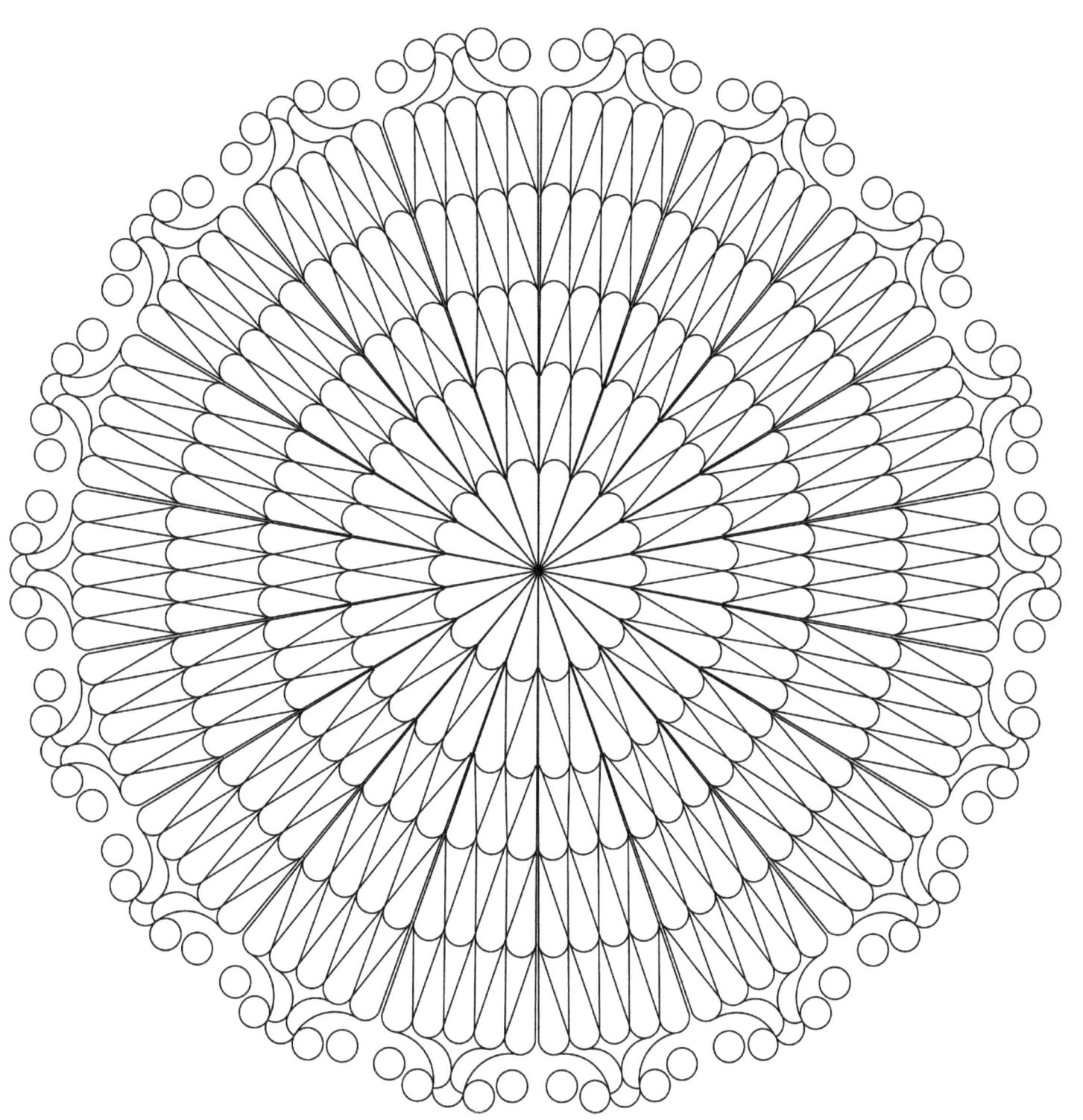

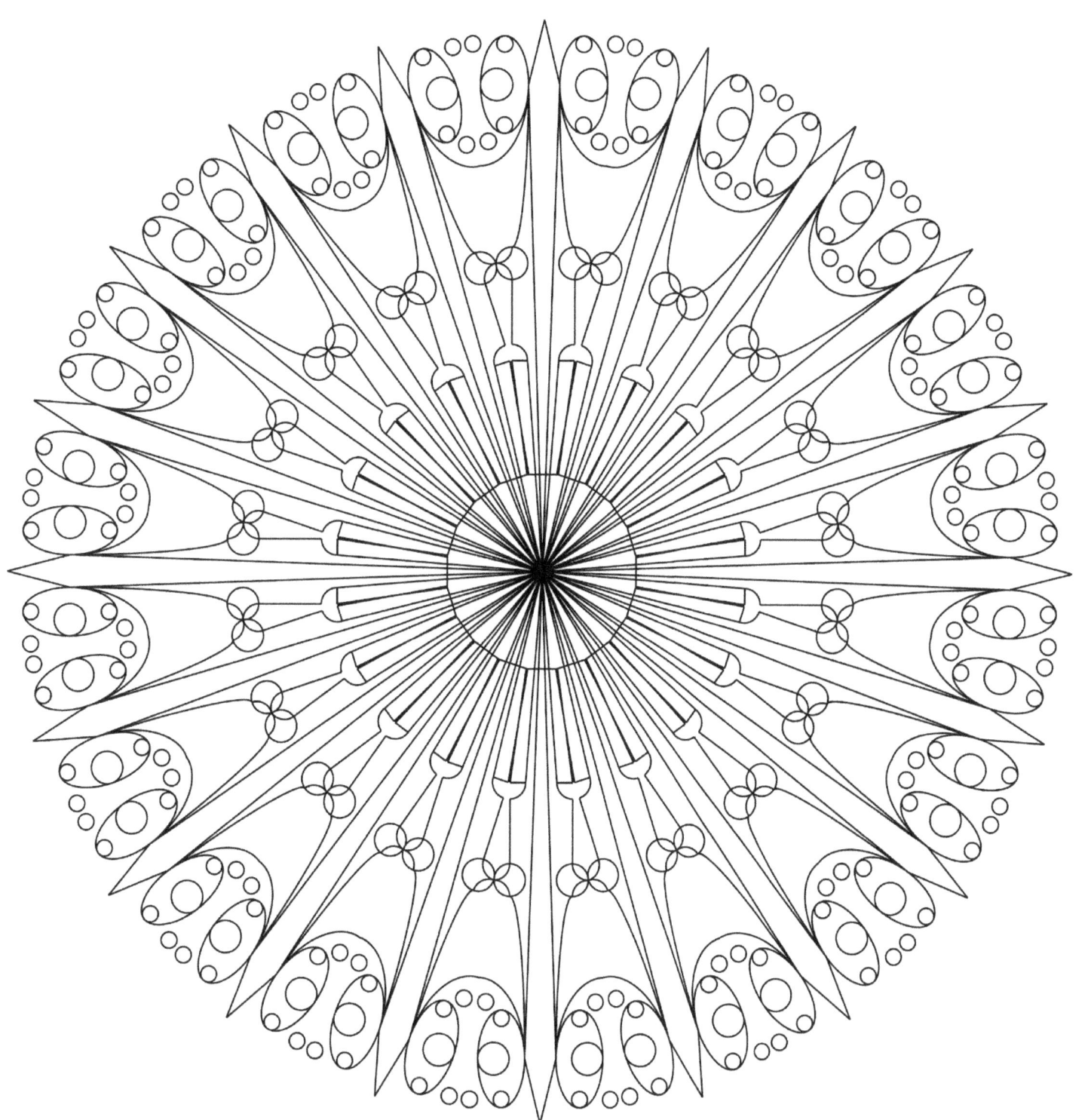

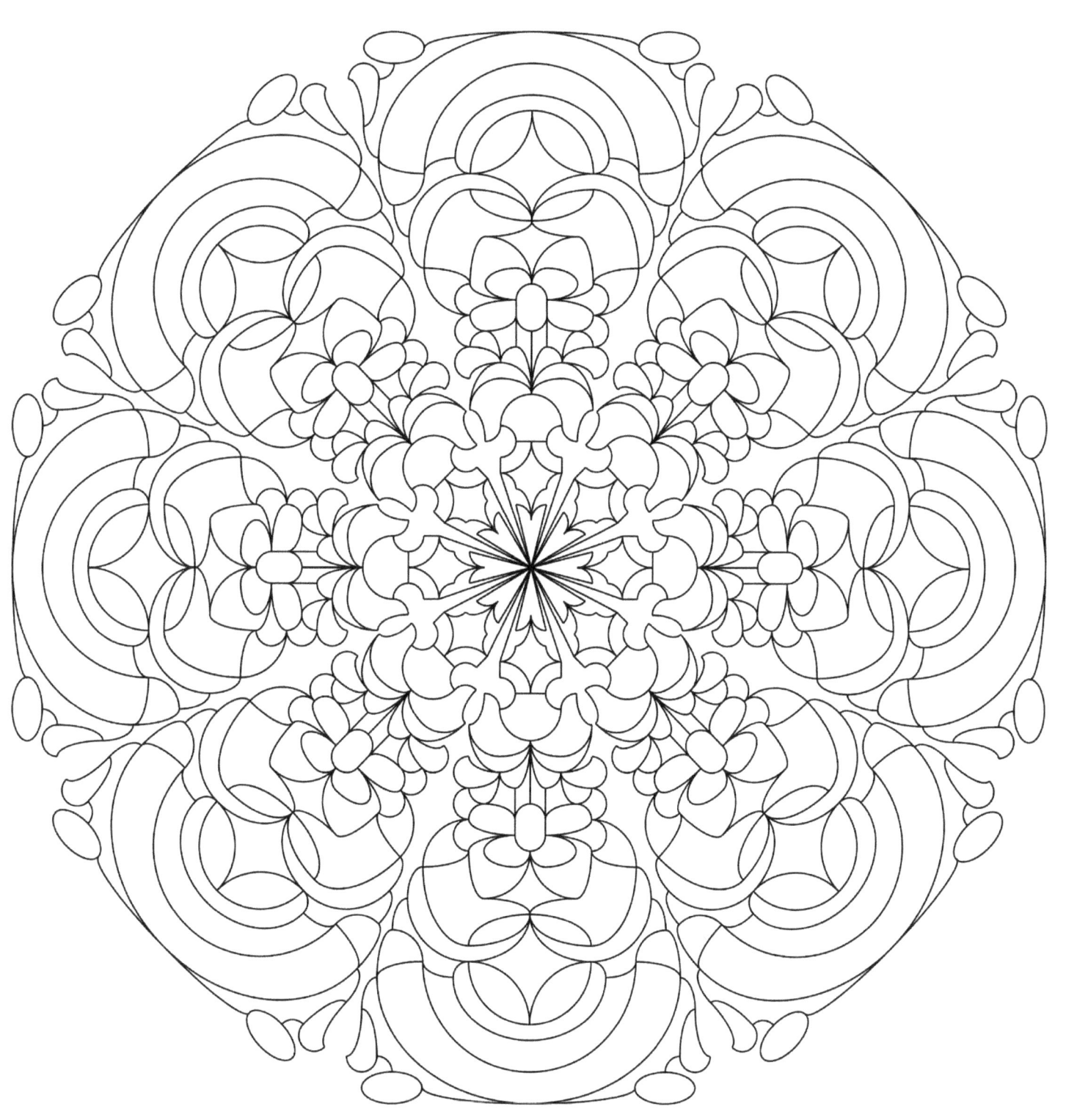

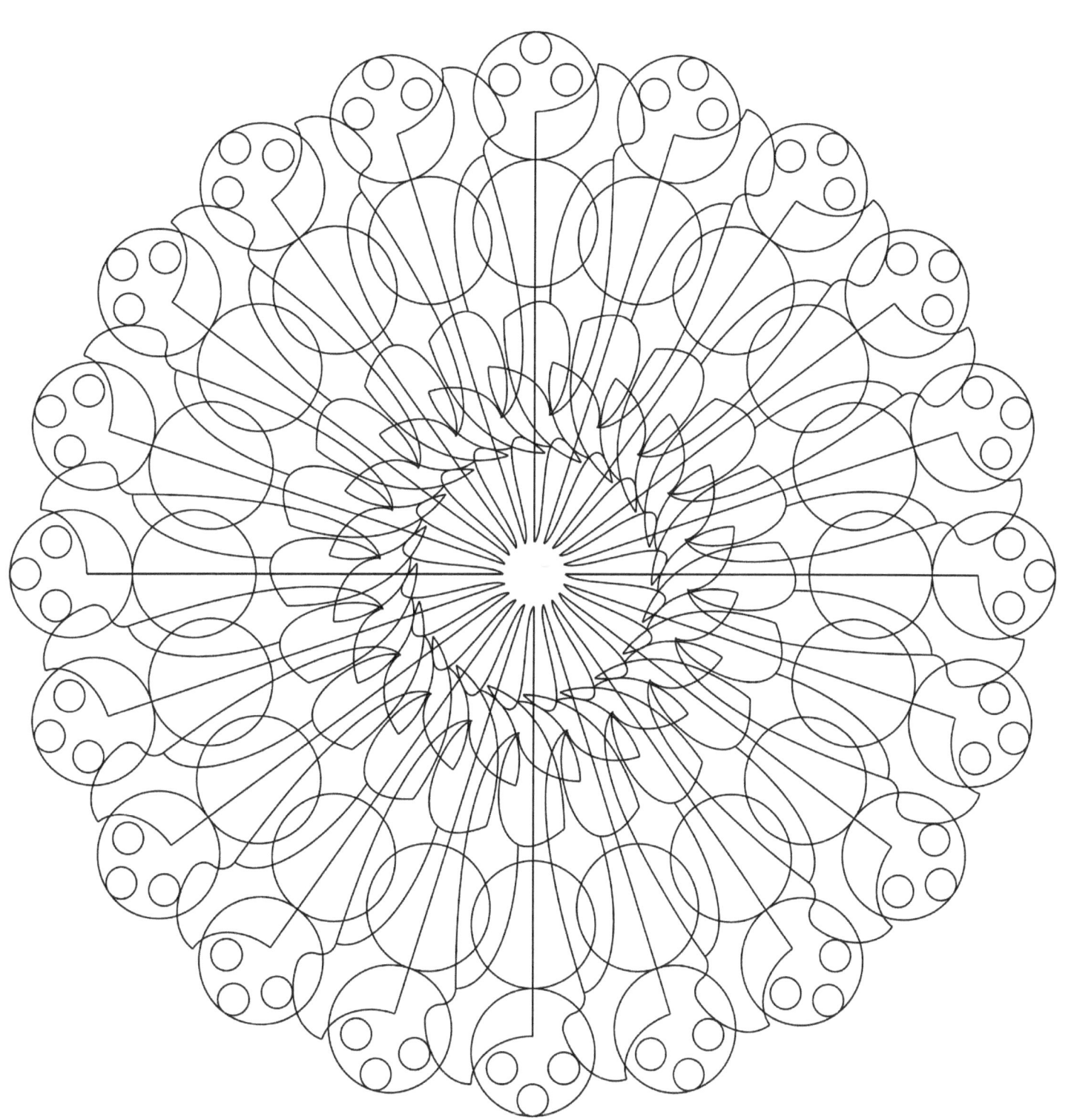

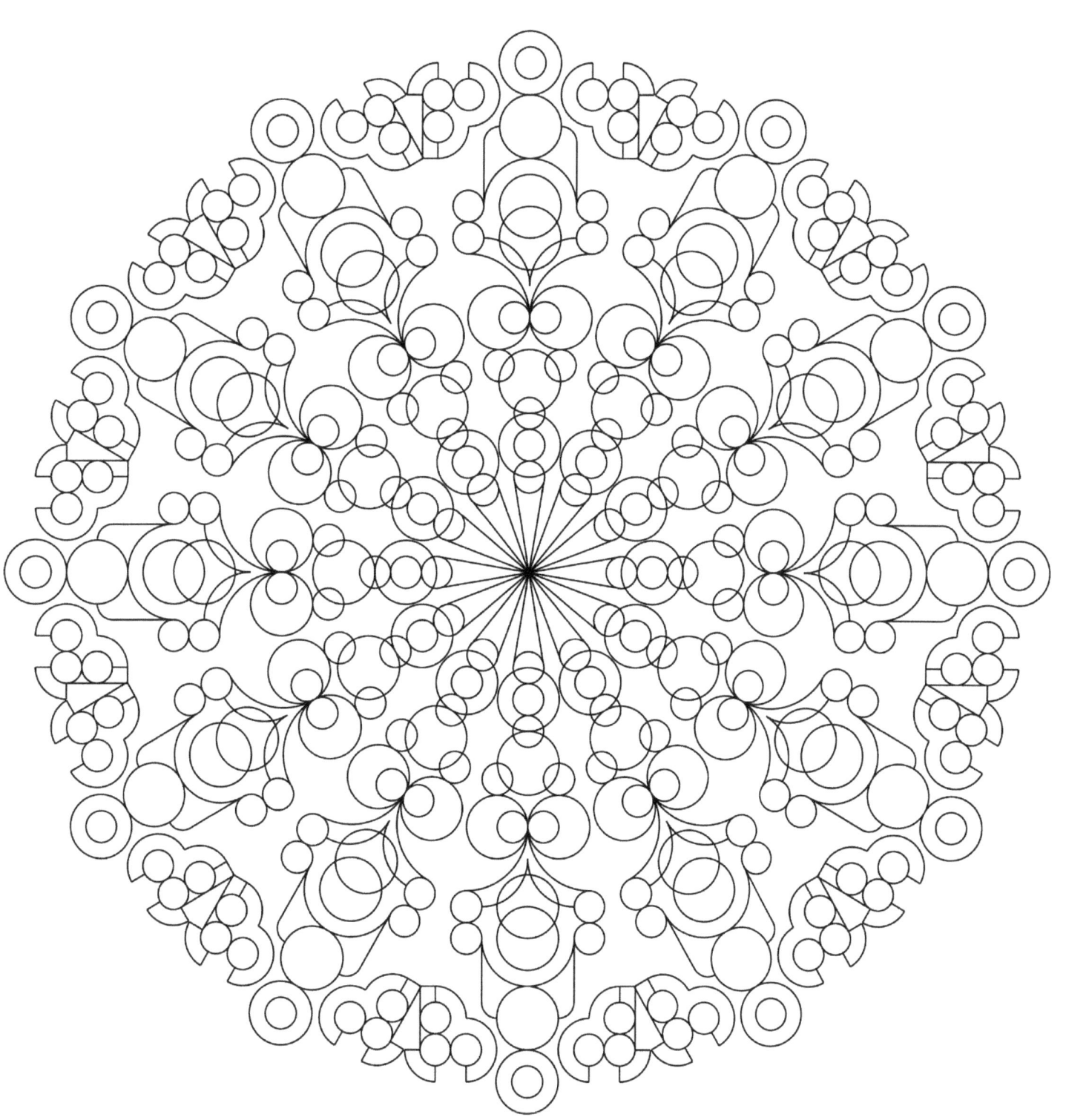

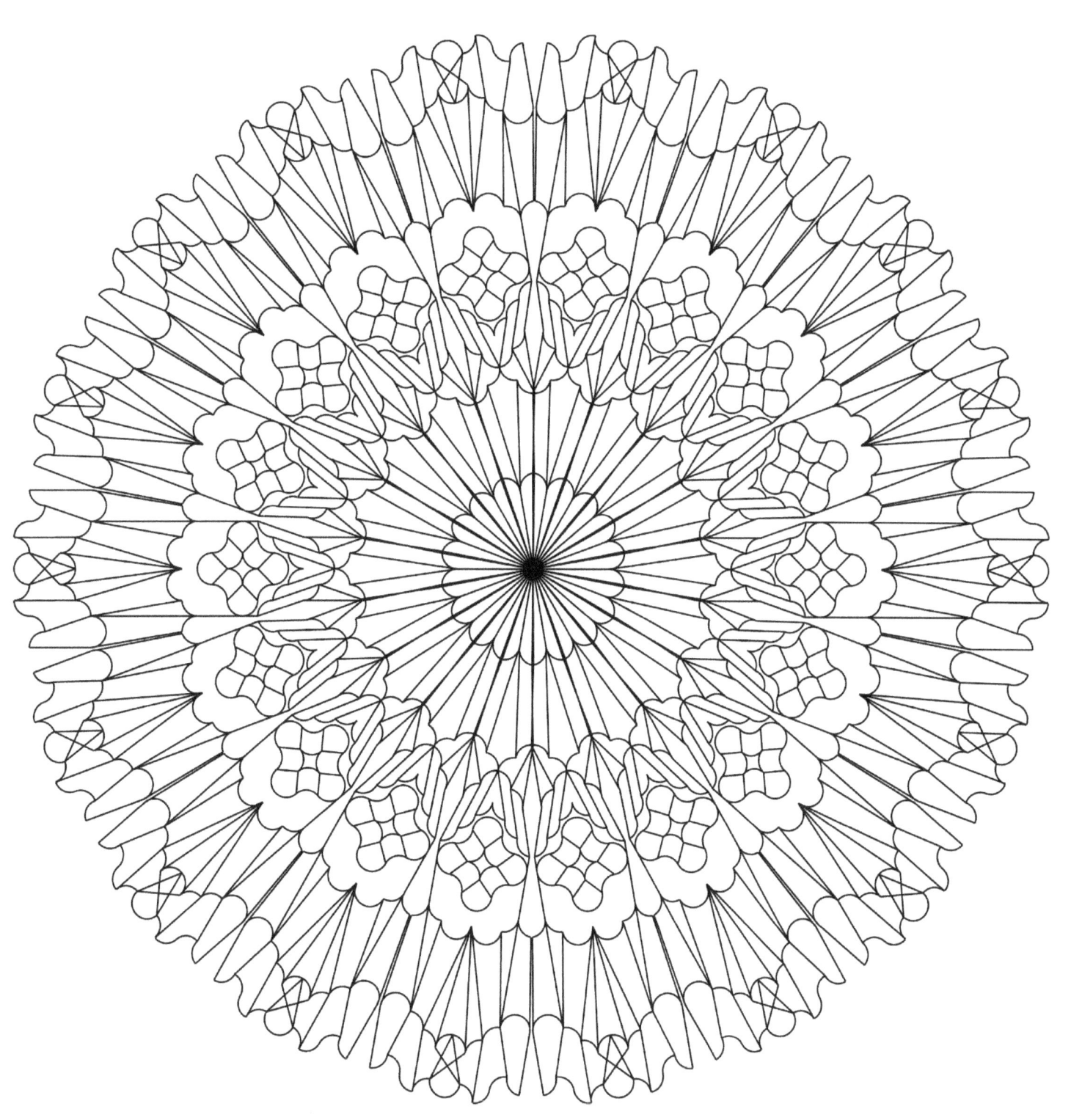

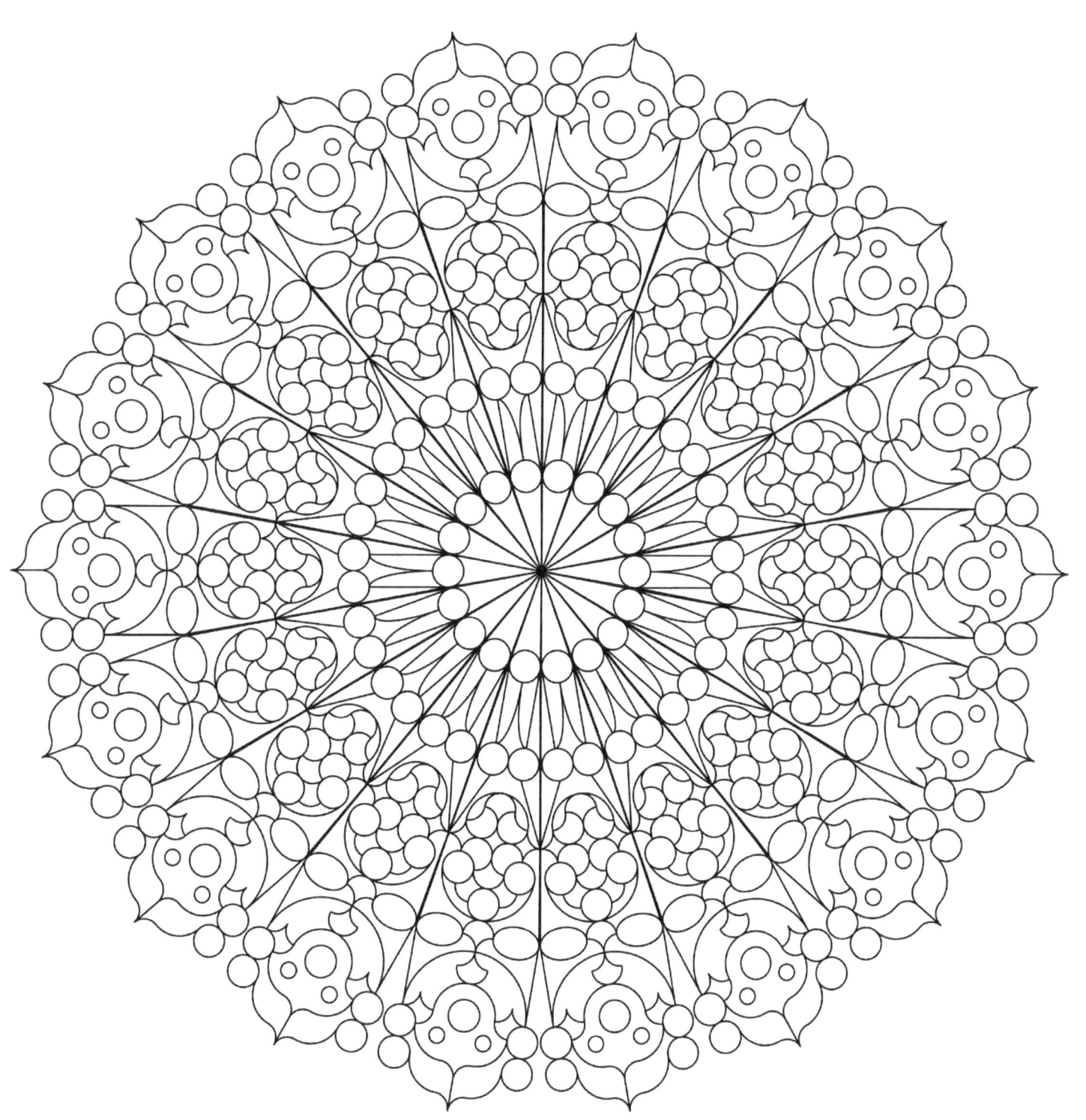

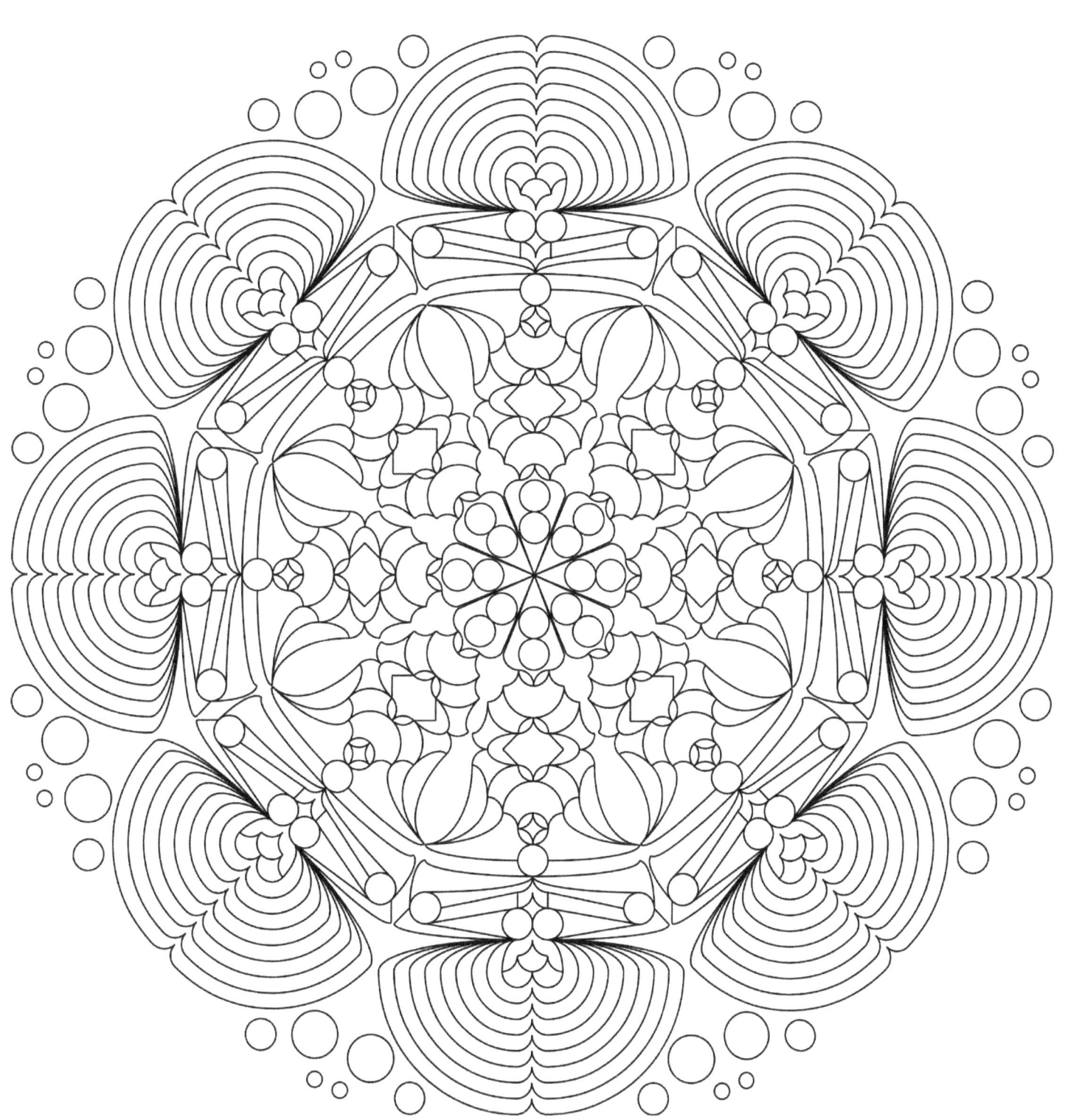

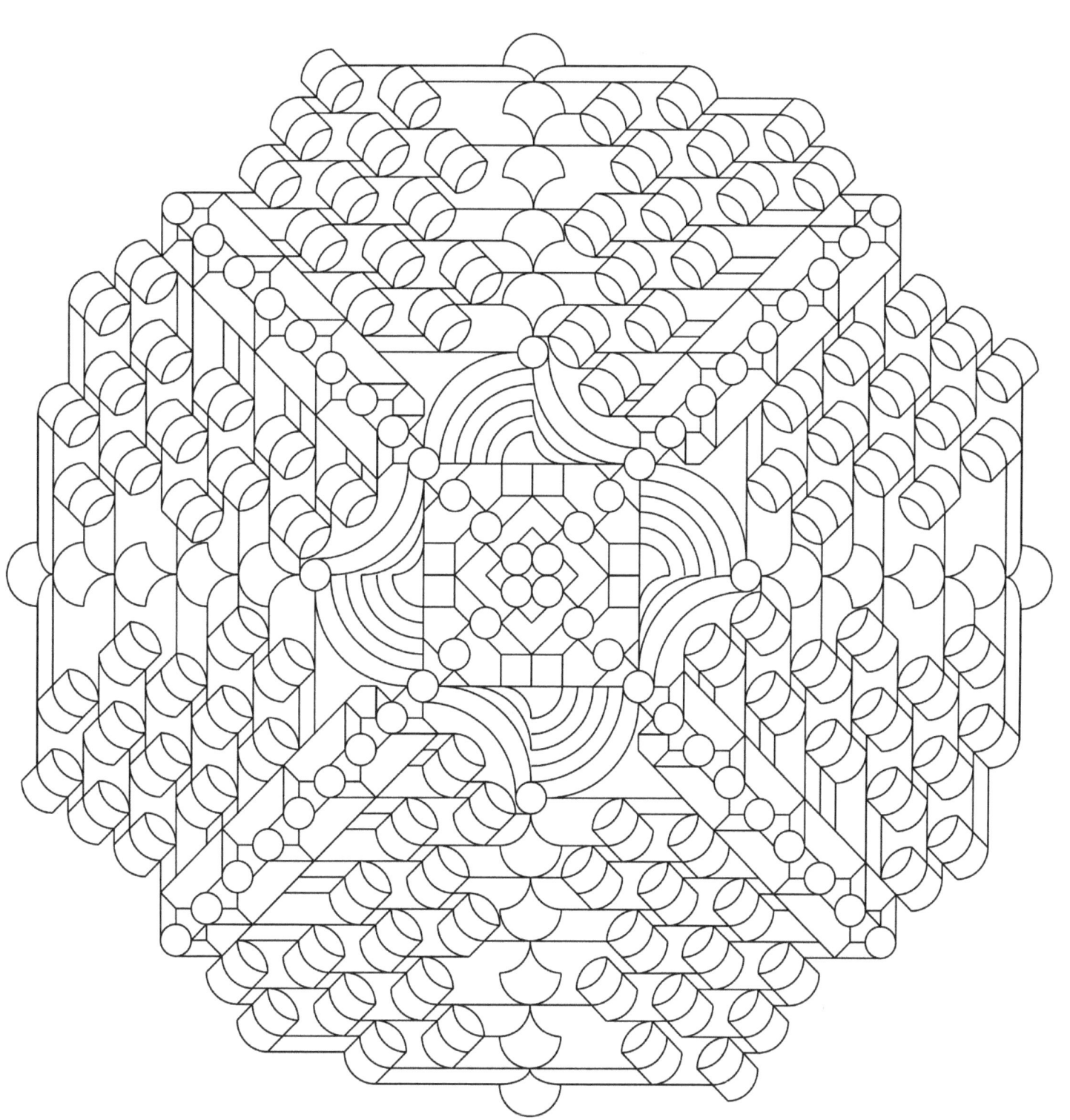

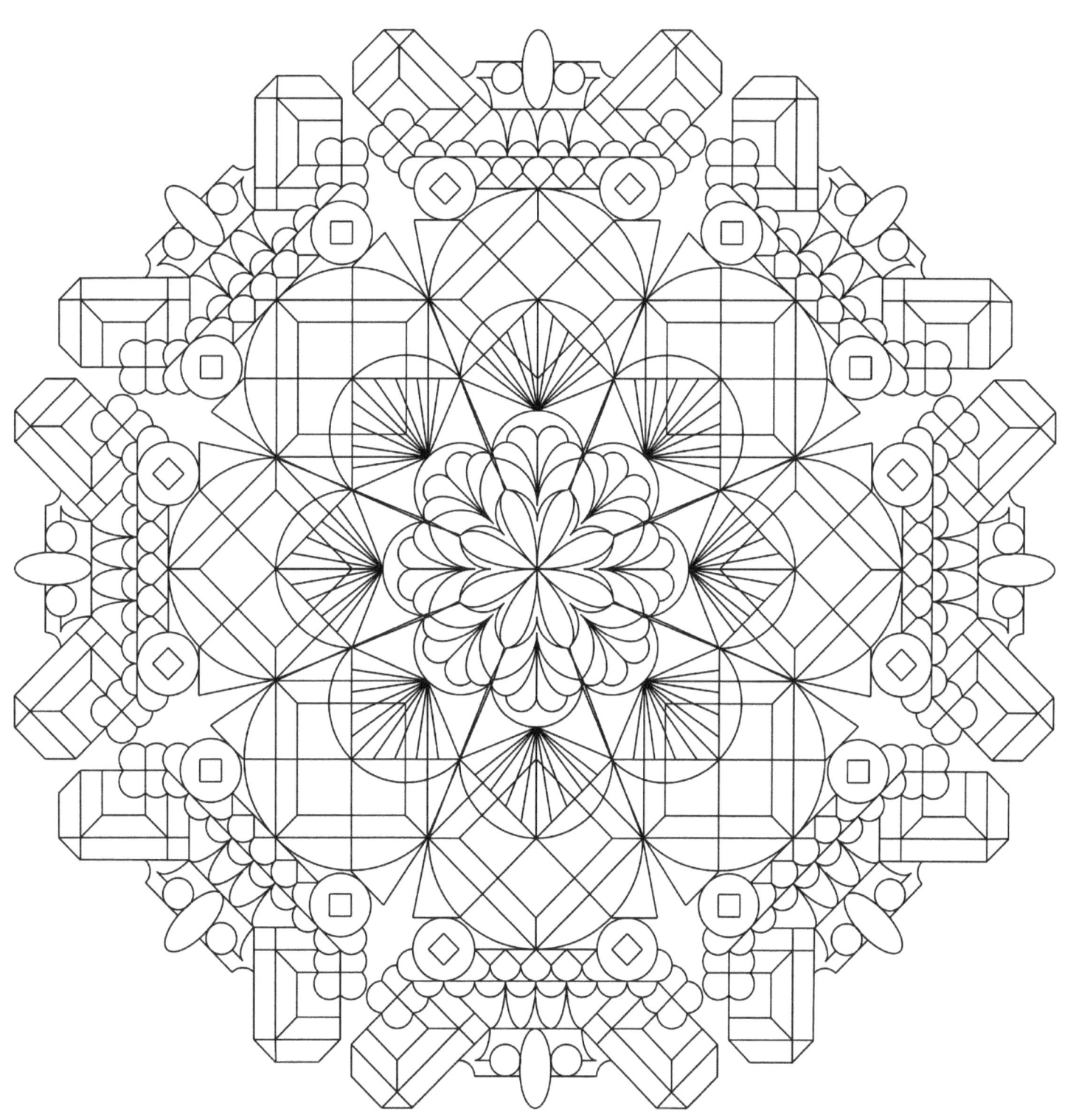

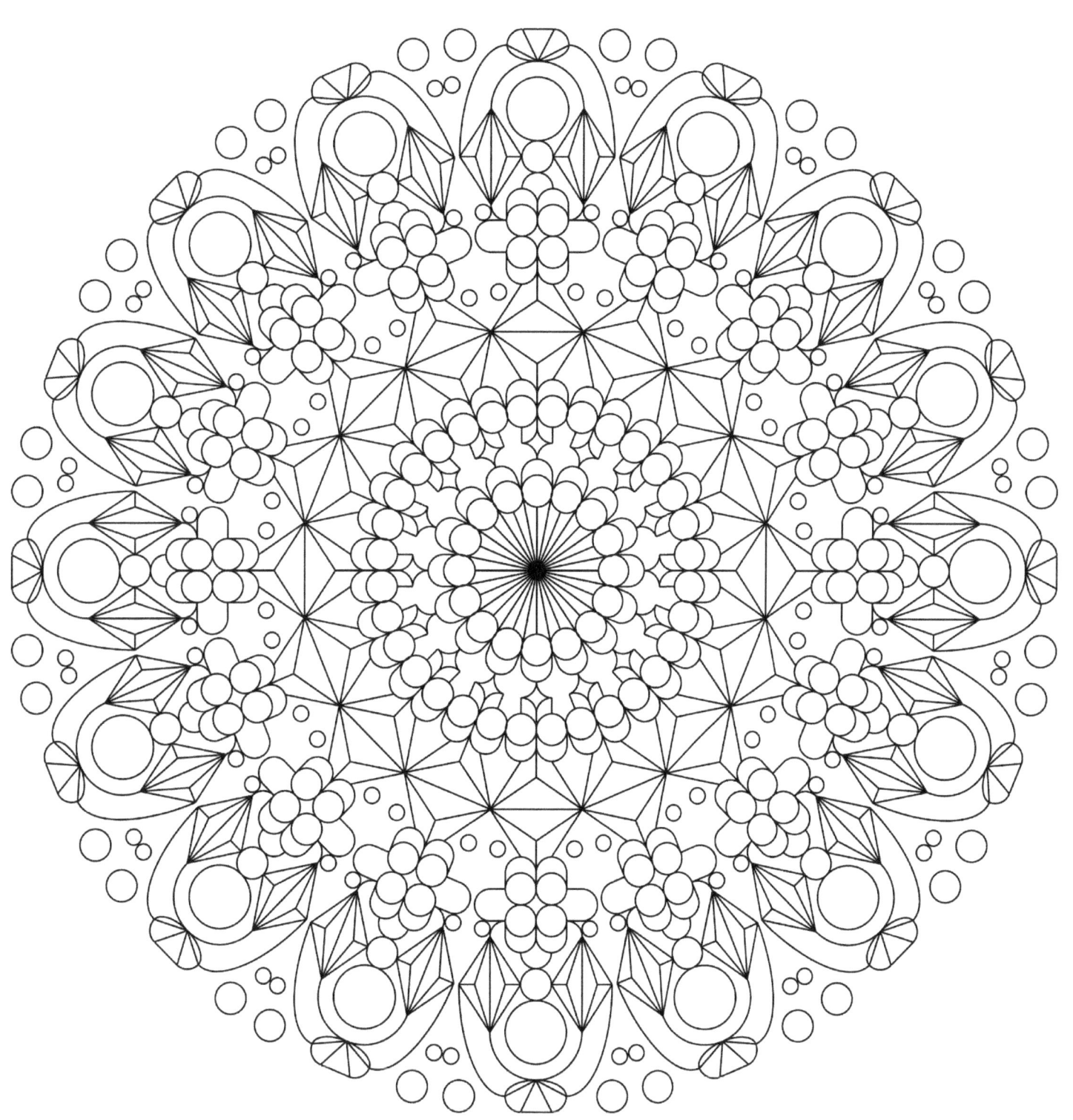

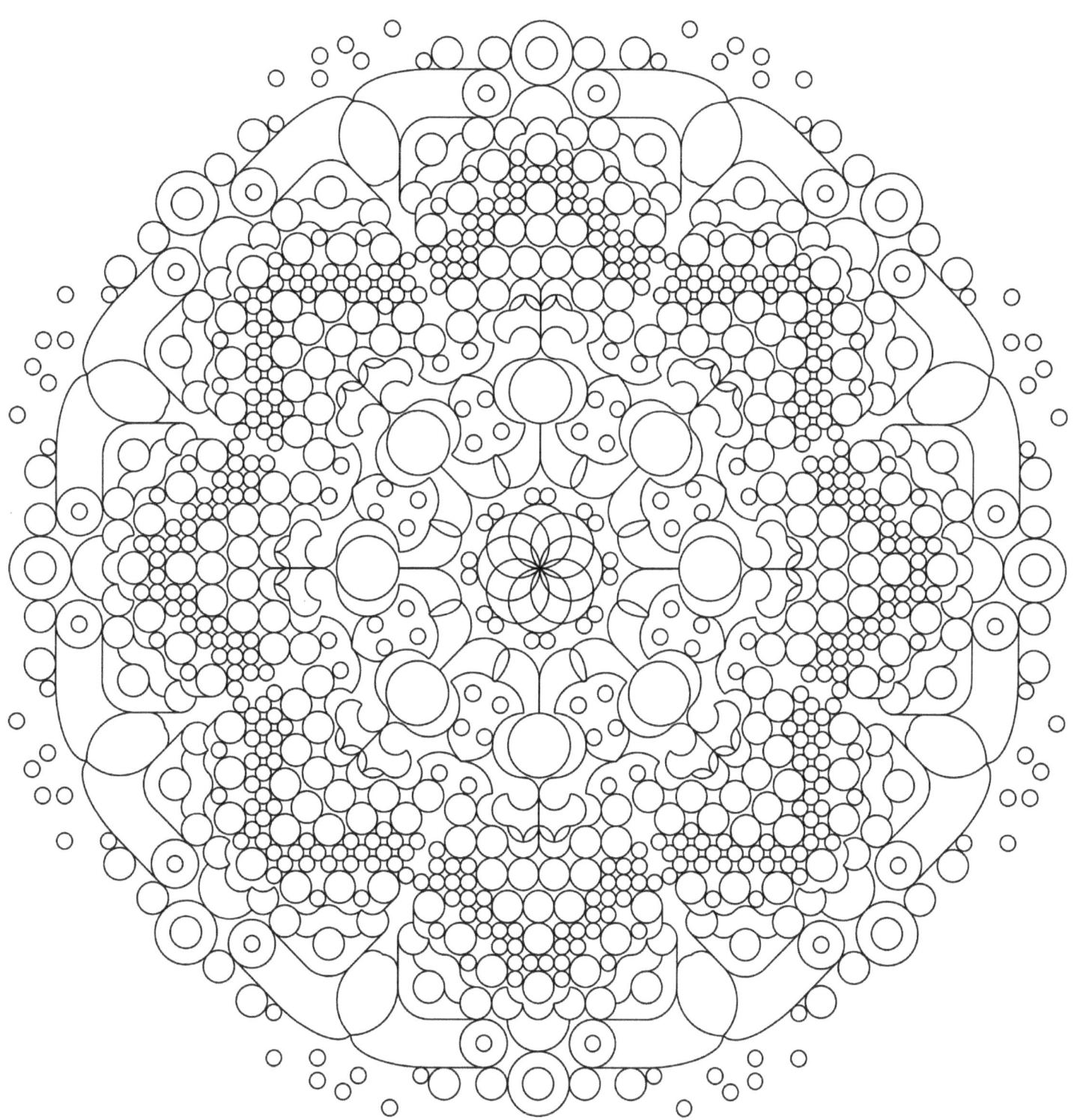

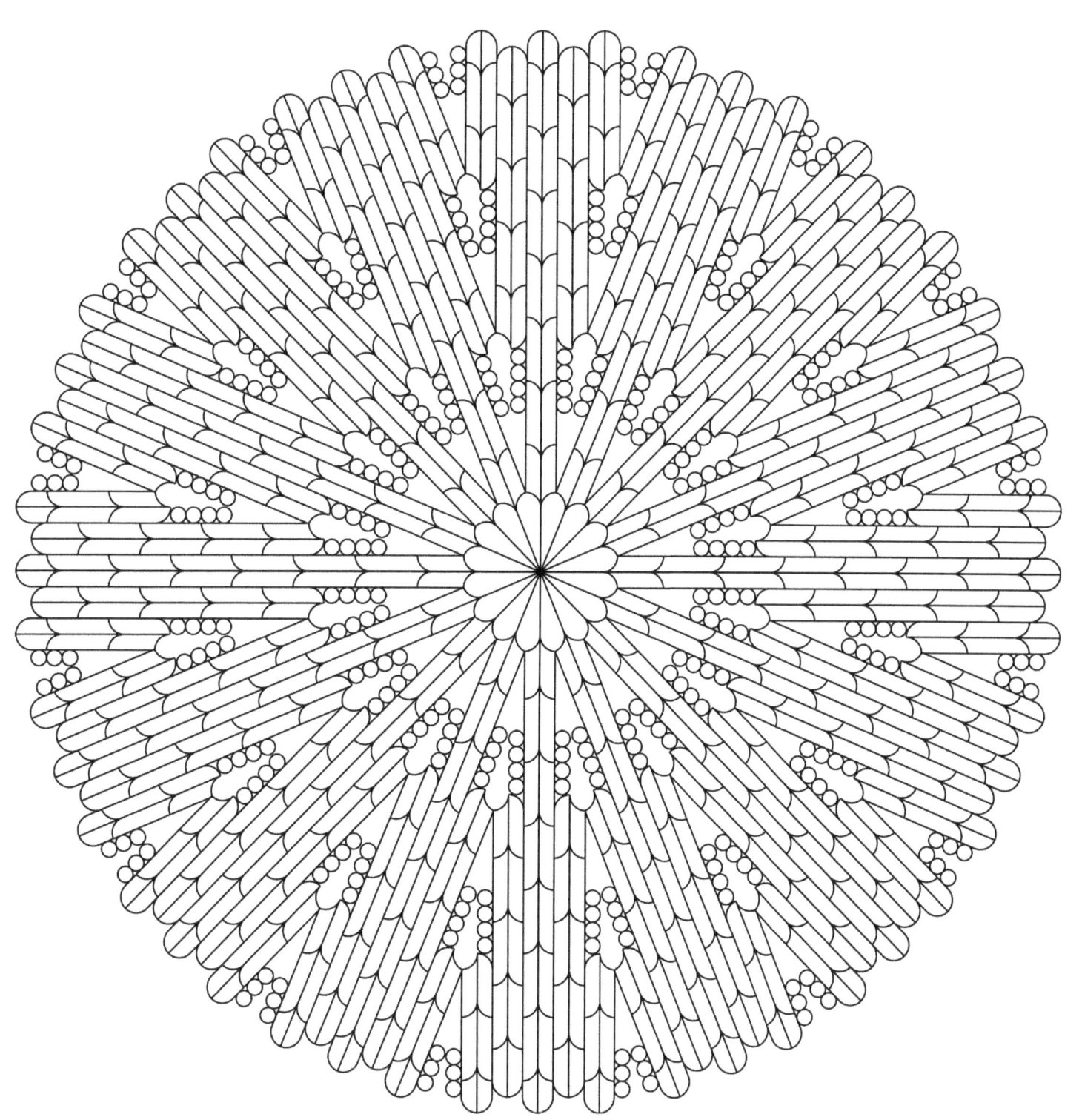

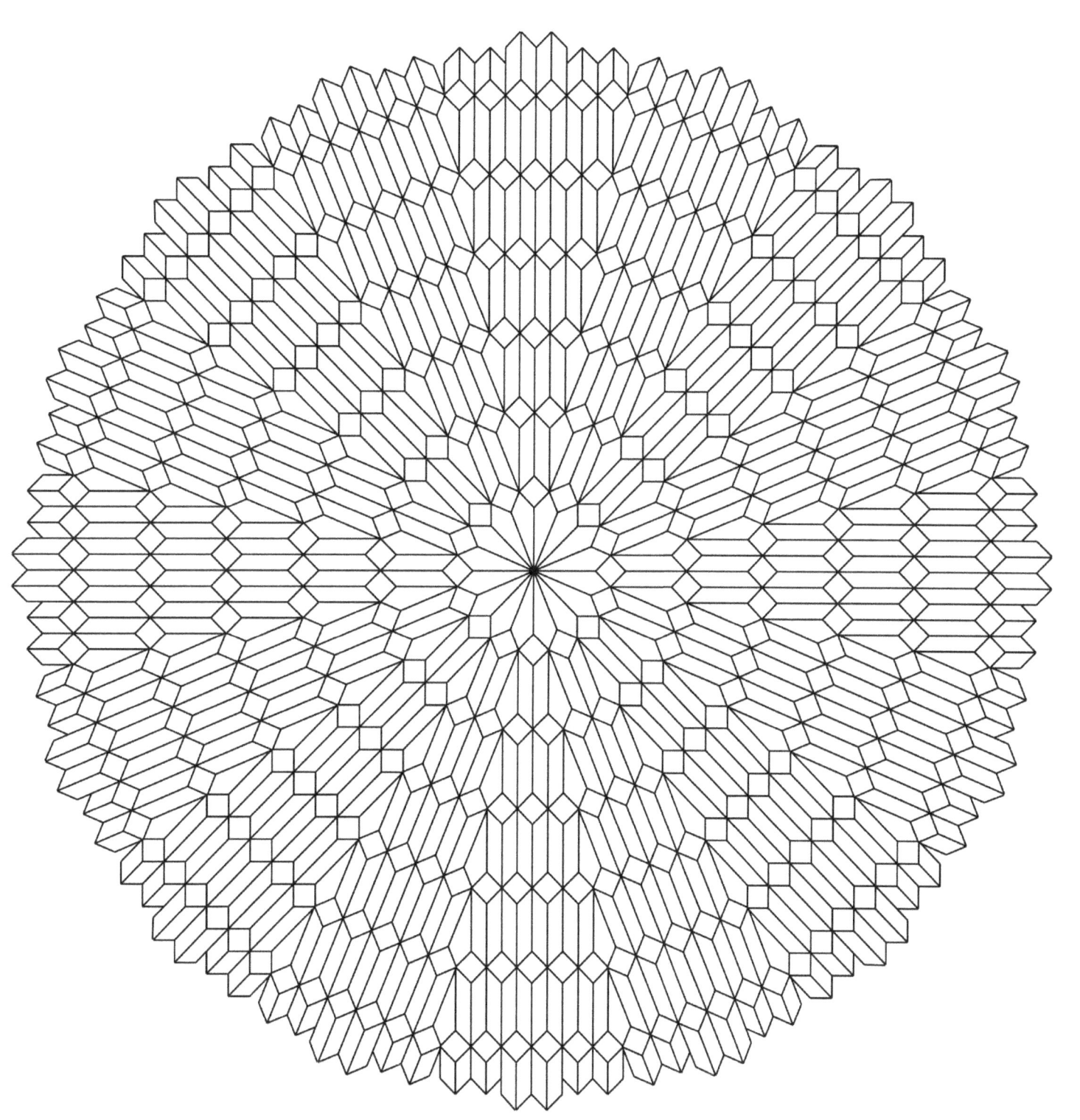

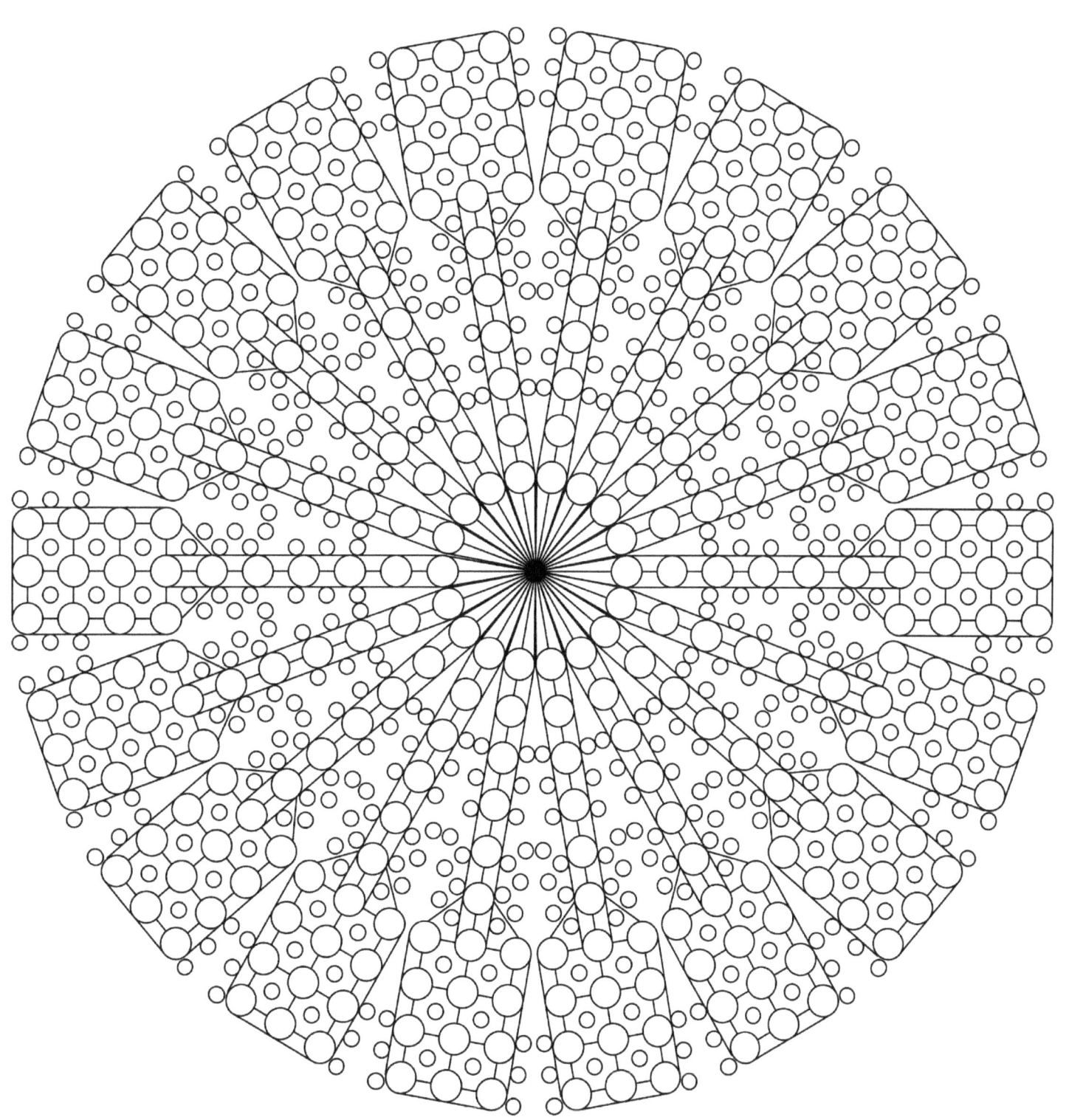

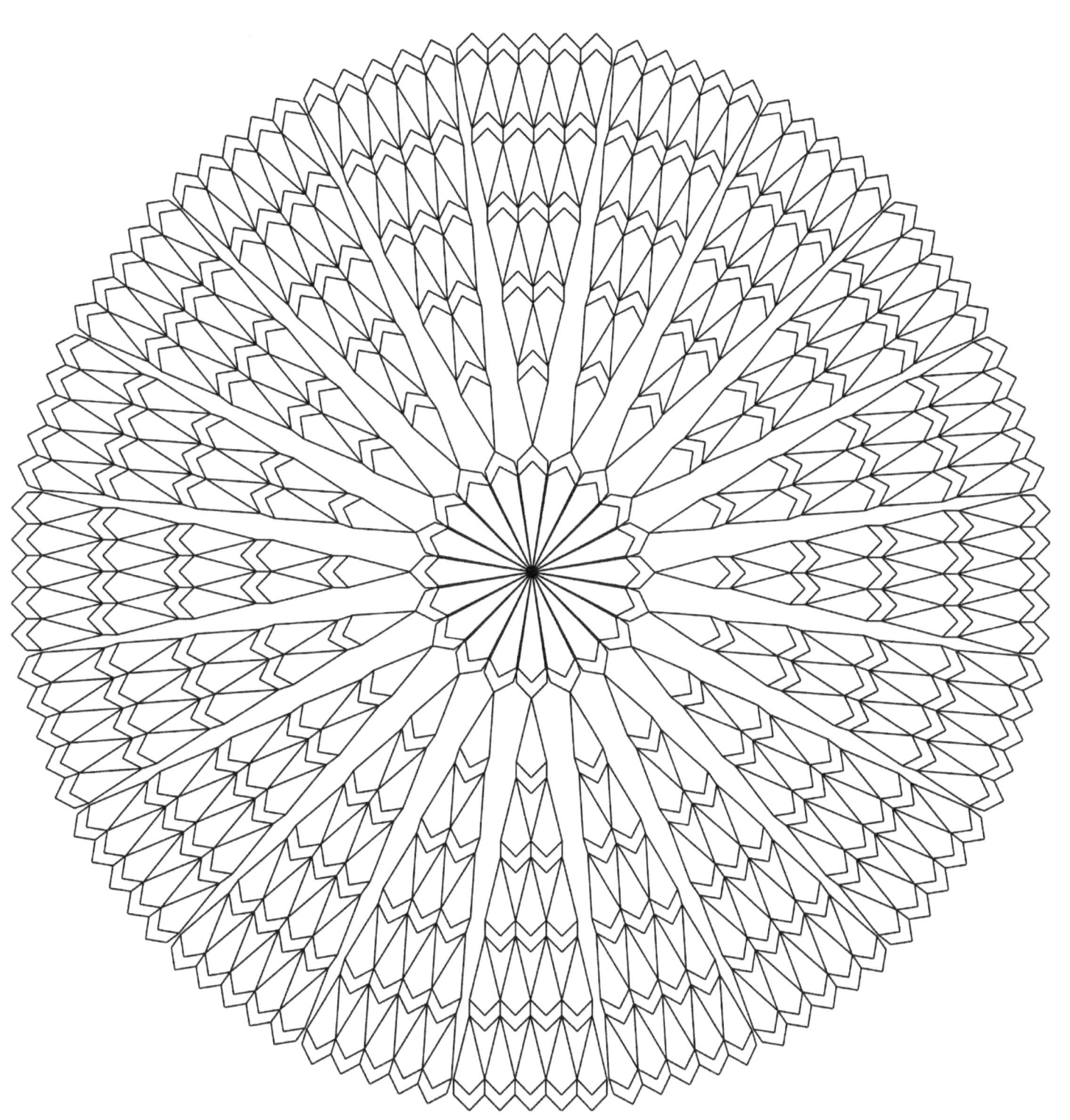

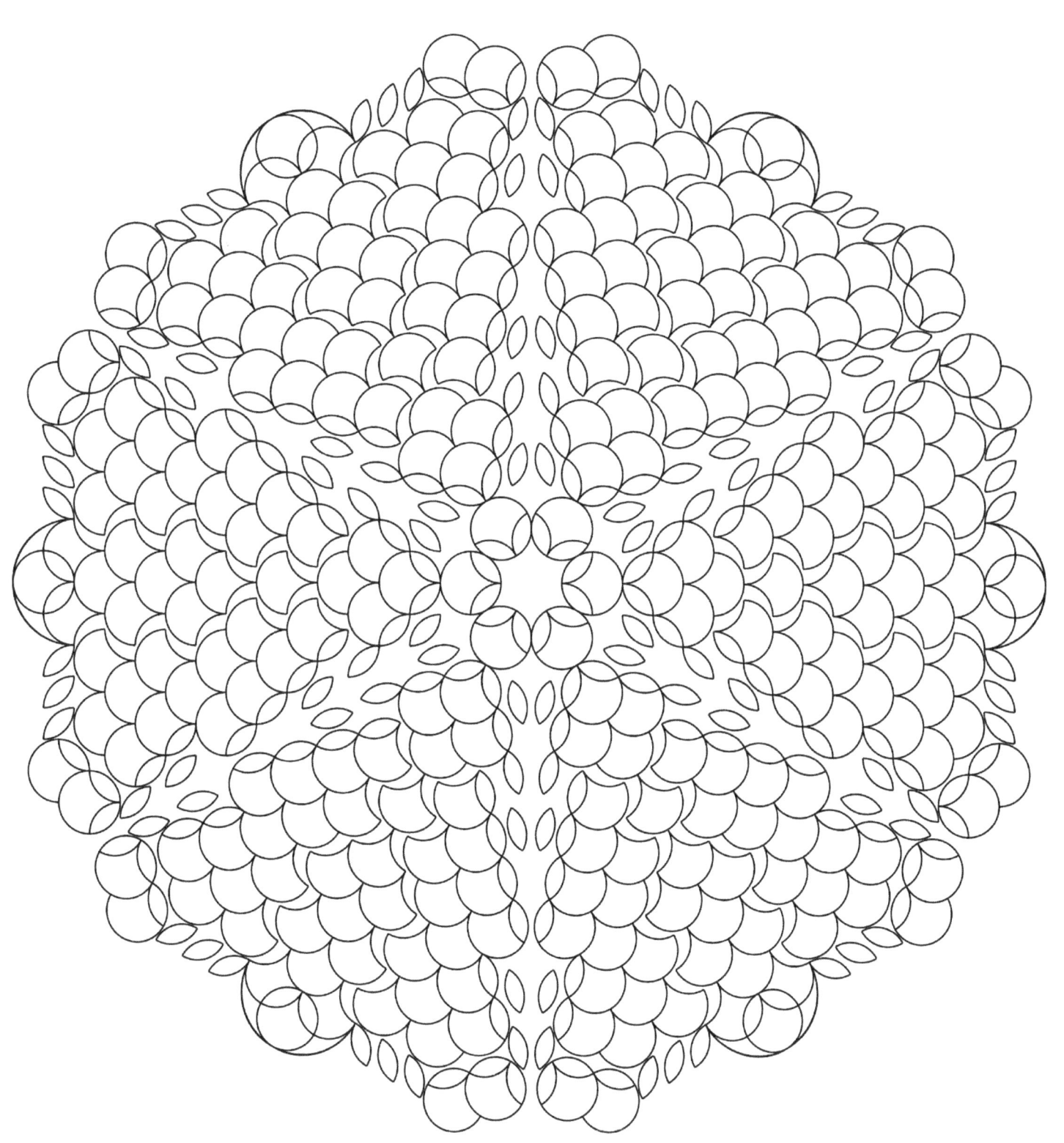

www.ingramcontent.com/pod-product-compliance
Lightning Source LLC
Chambersburg PA
CBHW080830180526
45168CB00006B/2629